SHORTHANDED SEAMANSHIP

By the same author

Start to Navigate
This excellent introduction to practical navigation is designed to appeal to young and old alike. Well illustrated, the book takes readers through the essentials so that they can try their hand at an early stage.
ISBN 0–229–11706–6

Basic Coastal Navigation
A well illustrated and simply written introduction to the subject of navigation and dead reckoning in coastal waters.
ISBN 0–229–11739–2

Basic Astro Navigation
The essentials of astro navigation are set out in a clear and readable way, with the aid of many explanatory diagrams. The navigator does not need special tables other than those found in any recent copy of Reed's Nautical Almanac.
ISBN 0–229–11740–6

Shorthanded Seamanship

CONRAD DIXON

Adlard Coles Nautical
London

Adlard Coles Nautical
An imprint of A & C Black (Publishers) Ltd
35 Bedford Row, London WC1R 4JH

First published in Great Britain by
Adlard Coles Nautical 1991

British Library Cataloguing in Publication Data

Dixon, Conrad
   Shorthanded seamanship.
   1. Sailing. Seamanship
   I. Title
   623.88223

   ISBN 0 7136 3433 2

Printed and bound in Great Britain by
Hollen Street Press Ltd, Slough

Contents

List of illustrations

x

Introduction

Boats tend to have full crews at holiday times and summer weekends, but at either end of the sailing season they are often encountered on the way out to a cruising ground, or heading back for a laying-up supper, with just a crew of two on board. As a consequence, it is when the weather is least favourable, the nights longer and the fewest hands are on board, that the greatest demand is made on seamanship skills. The intricate division of labour of the sunny days when it can be hard to find enough work for everyone to do is replaced by many tasks for the few; a mere couple to cope with raising and lowering sails, anchor work, coming alongside, steering, reading the weather and caring for the engine. This book has a single aim; to help a crew of two handle a yacht with the minimum of sweat and anxiety by directing their thoughts towards time and labour-saving wrinkles in order to get it right instinctively first time. Anyone can have a hard passage and arrive tired out and worried: readers who absorb the message that shorthanded is not at all the same as undermanned will never do so.

Conrad Dixon
January 1990

1   Casting off

Let us start with the simple case of two people in a boat moored alongside a quay with no wind or tidal movement to complicate matters. Four warps hold the craft as shown in Figure 1(a), and each is merely looped around its bollard on the quay so that all the work can be accomplished from the deck by letting go one end and pulling on the other. It is the kind of temporary mooring used when waiting for a lock to open, or when a visit has to be made to the harbour master's office to secure a berth, and it requires long warps. The bow and stern warps should be three times the length of the boat, and the springs twice its length. When it comes to casting off, the engine should be started and left running in neutral and a boathook placed handy amidships. One crew member will first take off the springs, coiling them as they come home. Then with one crew at the bow and one at the stern, the bow and stern warps are treated in the same way. A push with the butt end of the boathook and the craft is clear of the wall and ready to move ahead; one crew is at the wheel or tiller and the other deals with the fenders and warps. Shorthanded crews should always loop their lines in this fashion rather than tie them, because unmooring is more difficult when one person has to climb up a ladder to a quay, throw down the warps and then scramble on board again as the companion tries to hold the yacht in place near the ladder.

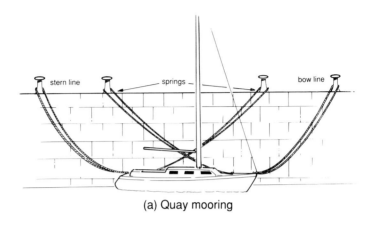

(a) Quay mooring

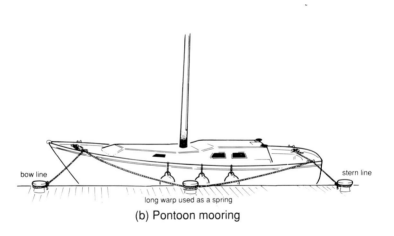

(b) Pontoon mooring

Figure 1 Moored alongside

The more familiar problem is that of leaving a floating pontoon. Here the lines or warps will either have
eyes or be knotted at the bollard end. In Figure 1(b)
the first step will be for both crew members to take
off, coil and stow the warp used as a two-part spring,

leaving the craft secured by bow and stern lines. It will be apparent right away that the crew handling the stern warp has the more difficult job because he or she will also have to take charge of the tiller or wheel and the engine controls. If the warp is long, heavy or wet it makes sense to remove it beforehand and use a last-minute line in its place. Figure 2(a) shows a light last-minute line that may be cast off one-handed; it can be short and not particularly strong because of the brief period of time it takes the strain. In Figure 1(b) the bow and stern warps have knotted loops, but where a boat is regularly sailed shorthanded it is advantageous to have spliced loops at the end of the major warps. That way, and with practice, the eyes may be 'flipped' off bollards with a sharp upwards jerk so that the forward crew need not venture on to the pontoon at all.

There is a special technique for withdrawing lines and warps from mooring rings. The key is to realize that the laws of physics dictate that a rope withdrawn through a ring behaves differently according to whether the ring is cemented in a horizontal or a vertical plane. As revealed in Figure 2(b), it is easier to pull a warp downwards from a horizontally fastened ringbolt; Figure 2(c) shows that it is easier from the friction aspect to pull a rope upwards from a vertically fitted bolt.

Countering wind and tide

Not much need be said about the effects of wind or tide when either acts to carry a boat clear from its berth, but things are likely to be awkward when a strong wind or tide is having a pinning effect on the beam of a moored craft. In Figure 3(a) the problem is that a strong wind is pushing the moored yacht (A) against a pontoon and

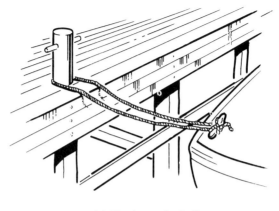

(a) The last-minute line

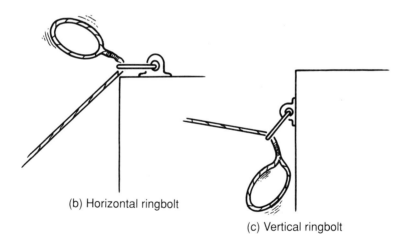

(b) Horizontal ringbolt

(c) Vertical ringbolt

Figure 2 Letting go

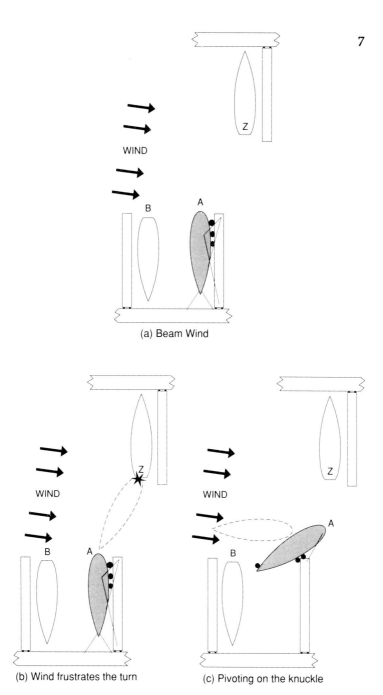

(a) Beam Wind

(b) Wind frustrates the turn

(c) Pivoting on the knuckle

Figure 3 Leaving a pontoon berth with a beam wind

room for manœuvre is strictly limited by an adjacent pontoon with another craft on it (Z). Motoring astern is likely to lead to the situation in Figure 3(b) where the boat has got out of its berth, but has been unable to turn head to wind before drifting across to strike the moored yacht (Z). The solution is outlined in Figure 3(c) where the crew has used the stern line to pivot the boat on the knuckle of the finger pier and then, when heading into the wind, has cast off and gone ahead safely. Note that in Figure 3(c) the crew has transferred fenders amidships as the stern warp has been eased out, while another fender has moved on to the starboard bow to prevent any impact damage with boat (B) sharing the berth.

Leaving a pile mooring

Pile moorings can be difficult to leave when the tide is whipping through the posts and heaping up on the beam of moored craft. Apart from waiting for slack water, the best option for a shorthanded crew is to carry out a long line by dinghy in the direction the tide is coming from and pass it round an object that gives purchase, so that the boat can come head to tide with rudder and propeller giving proper control. The situation in Figure 4 is typical. The moored yacht in Figure 4(a) is sagging down-tide on her lines. If the couple on board merely cast off the lines and supporting buoys, and try to motor through the posts, it seems likely that the tide will sweep the boat on to the pile in the lower right-hand corner of the diagram. A fully manned yacht could risk it because there are plenty of

Figure 4 Leaving a pile mooring with a beam wind or tide

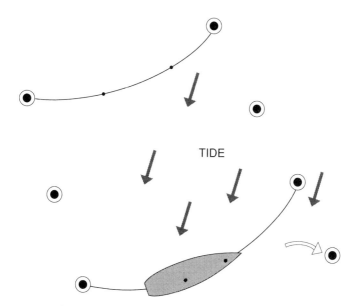

(a) Tide makes passage through piles difficult

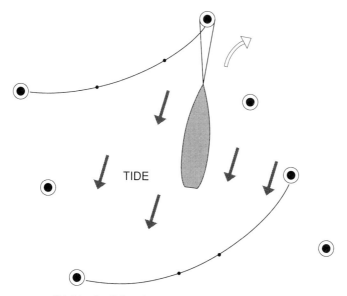

(b) Haul-off line brings yacht head to tide,
and alternative exit is used.

hands to bear off, but shorthanders dare not. In Figure 4(b) one of those on board the moored yacht has gone off in a dinghy and passed a light haul-off line round an up-tide pile, and brought the free end back on board. Using the foredeck winch, the yacht can be brought head to tide with the engine in neutral while the permanent lines and buoys are cast off. Once clear and facing into the tide, the yacht can go ahead with perfect safety and control. Reeling in the haul-off rope after one end has been let go has to be accomplished smartly, in case the boat runs over it and fouls the sterngear. This technique may also be employed when the tide is reasonably neutral and it is the wind that is on the beam instead.

Leaving a berth with tide or wind astern

When wind or tide are acting on the stern, and the yacht is in a tight space between two others, it is essential for a small crew to make use of all the low cunning they possess. Going ahead from the moored position in Figure 5(a) will only lead to bumps and scratches. The proper solution is sketched out in Figure 5(b), where one crew member is standing by the head spring, having let go all the other warps while the other puts the rudder to port and goes slow ahead on the engine. The effect is to hold the bow in and force the stern out; when the hull is at an angle of about 30° to the quay the flowing tide gets in between the two and increases the leverage. With the stern well clear, the headspring may be let go and brought in as the

Figure 5 Leaving a berth with tide astern

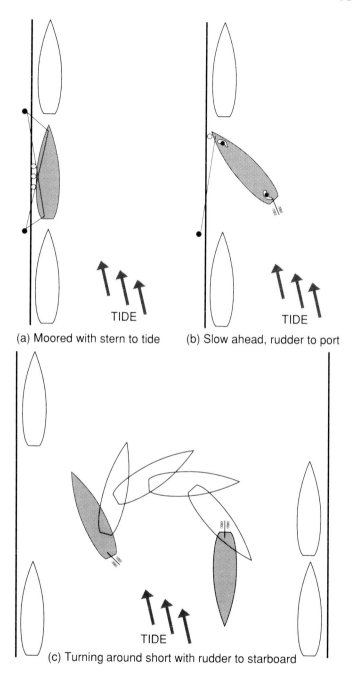

(a) Moored with stern to tide

(b) Slow ahead, rudder to port

(c) Turning around short with rudder to starboard

rudder goes amidships, and the yacht goes slow astern to end up in the position shown on the left-hand side of Figure 5(c).

In this case, the intention after casting-off is to breast the incoming tide, so the crew member at the helm puts the rudder to starboard and begins to turn round short to starboard at low speed. Where space is limited, the U-turn may be made with the helm held to starboard, and going alternately ahead and astern on the engine. With strong wind or tide causing a great deal of drift it might be necessary to have the rudder to starboard while going ahead, and to port when going astern, but most modern boats are responsive enough to make this merely optional. A great deal depends on the paddlewheel or propwalk effect associated with a particular boat, since the sideways push from the propeller is much more pronounced with some types. However, with practice these kinds of manœuvres become child's play once it is clear which is the most efficient way to turn.

Three pieces of advice are worth retaining. The fender at the bow in Figure 5(b) is a must, and it is as well to spare the engine by pausing in neutral briefly between ahead and astern and *not* doing everything at maximum revolutions. Excessive wrenching at throttle or tiller will be counter-productive, since all craft respond best to smooth alternations of speed and direction, while crew morale soars if it can be seen that the individual at the blunt end knows what he or she is doing.

Having covered the routine method of getting under way with a two-person crew, it is time to explore the finer points of technique.

Starboard side to

Right-handed propellers, which most yachts have, tend to push the stern to starboard at the early stages of a departure from a berth, and when the wind is also pinning the boat to the shore it is essential to use backspring and boathook together to unglue craft berthed on their starboard sides. In Figure 6(a) the two crew members are shown working out of a tight corner. The backspring has been retained after all other warps have been removed, and the person up forward is pushing the bow out with the boathook. When the bow is clear, the vessel can go slowly ahead as the backspring is recovered. Note that a fender has been positioned right aft on to starboard side to act as the fulcrum for the thrust of the boathook.

Winding

Where a boat has insufficient room to turn round short under engine after leaving its berth, it will be necessary to turn it round by hand to face the right way *before* moving off from that berth. Known as 'winding', the method relies on exploiting the push of wind or tide to alter the heading of the bow by 180°. In Figure 6(b)1 the crew have reduced the holding warps to a backspring and long bowline, passing the latter outside everything to the quay. The bow is pushed out by one crew member exerting pressure on the starboard quarter, while the other pulls on the backspring until the boat has reached the position shown in Figure 6(b)2. The wind now assists the turning process, and the yacht finishes up as shown in Figure 6(b)3, facing the exit after being turned end-for-end.

WIND

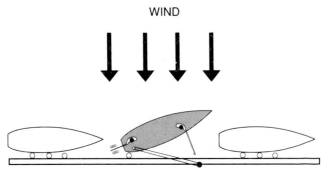

(a) Starboard side to with a beam wind; boathook
and backspring in use

WIND

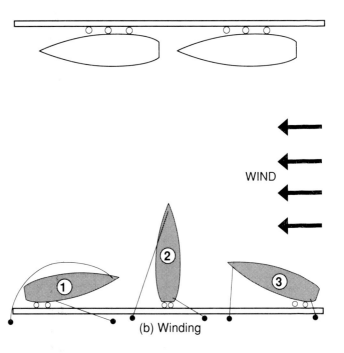

(b) Winding

Figure 6 Starboard side to, and winding

There is a second reason for having winding as a weapon in the armoury of a shorthanded crew. On a windy day the recovery of warps by the person at the stern of the craft immediately after casting off takes some seconds, and meanwhile the yacht is drifting with no one tending the throttle or moving the rudder, so that some ground is inevitably lost. It is quite possible, therefore, for the tide or wind to carry the boat into an awkward corner without the crew being immediately aware of it. The only sure way of avoiding this dilemma is to turn the boat manually while it is still attached to something solid, so that it can be pointing at the exit before departure.

Unrafting

Cruising boats often have to moor three or four deep on a quay or pontoon, and in places such as Weymouth or Courseulles, where rafts form and dissolve daily, a certain amount of skill is required when inside boats want to cast off before those on the outside are ready to leave. In Figure 7(a) three craft are shown properly moored with head and stern ropes, springs and breast ropes; it is the middle one that wants to get away first. In Figure 7(b) the two-man crew have made a start by loosening up the raft and have taken off the springs on both sides, and the breast ropes to the outside boat. In Figure 7(c) one crew member has taken off the breast lines to the inside boat while the other has run the stern line of the outside boat round the bow of the middle boat, so that the latter can work clear. At this point one crew member is on board the middle yacht; the other is either on the quay or on the outside boat pulling it in and making it fast to the inboard boat as shown in Figure 7(d). If you are very lucky there will be people on the other craft to help out. Quite often, however, the crew member who pulls in and secures the outboard boat will have to work alone, while his partner circles around in the departing yacht before coming back to pick him up.

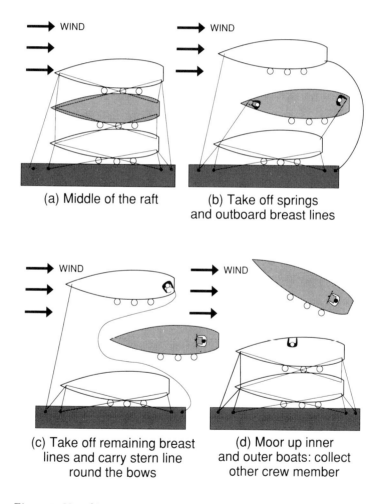

(a) Middle of the raft

(b) Take off springs and outboard breast lines

(c) Take off remaining breast lines and carry stern line round the bows

(d) Moor up inner and outer boats: collect other crew member

Figure 7 Unrafting

Three more points about unrafting should be made. A great deal of stress may be averted if the various parts of the raft get together as it is formed and rank themselves, from the outside, in order of proposed departure time – although it is only fair to say this may conflict with that other general order of ranking in which the heaviest yachts are nearest the shore and the lightest are on the outside. Figure 7 shows the boat getting away head to current: where a raft faces stern to current or tide, it will be the head ropes that are passed around the stern of the departing vessel. In this latter instance, be careful about using the engine too soon and be quite sure that no loose lines ensnare the propeller. Finally, do not neglect to position the fenders of the remaining members of the raft in the manner in which you would expect to find your own after an absence.

Sailing off a pontoon

The subject of hoisting and setting sails is dealt with comprehensively in Chapter 3. What is sketched in here is the use of sails to get a yacht away from an outer pontoon or quay when the wind is favourable. In essence, this is possible whenever the wind is parallel to the berth or blows offshore, and the four parts of Figure 8 show what has to be done. In Figure 8(a) the wind is from dead ahead at the berth; both sails are hoisted, and the jib is backed to get the head off. In part 4 of Figure 8(a) the jib has gone over to starboard, the main has been hardened in and the yacht is moving off close-hauled. In Figure 8(b) the wind is on the port bow. After the hoisted jib fills, the lines are let go, the main brought in and, again, the yacht moves away close-hauled. With a quartering wind the

Figure 8 Sailing off a pontoon

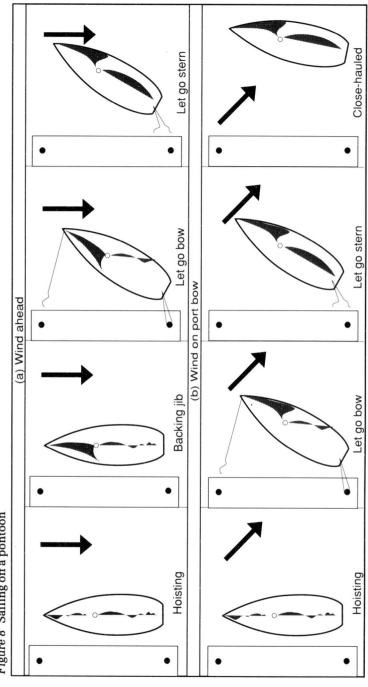

(a) Wind ahead

Hoisting   Backing jib   Let go bow   Let go stern

(b) Wind on port bow

Hoisting   Let go bow   Let go stern   Close-hauled

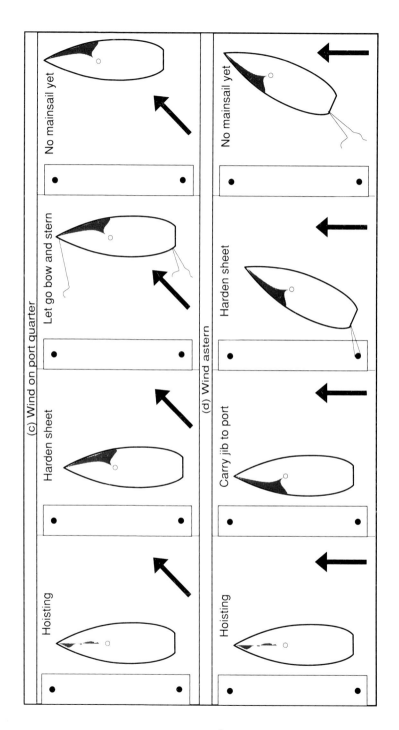

(c) Wind on port quarter

Hoisting | Harden sheet | Let go bow and stern | No mainsail yet

(d) Wind astern

Hoisting | Carry jib to port | Harden sheet | No mainsail yet

jib alone is brought into play, and Figure 8(c) shows the yacht drawing steadily away as the lines are paid out. Why no mainsail? This is because a hoisted main would have the effect of forcing the bows back into the pontoon. A stern wind means that the hoisted and flapping jib is carried over to the port side, so that when the sheet is hardened it will exert a turning force and push the bows out from the berth – as in Figure 8(d). In this last manœuvre it is necessary to keep a line on to the pontoon until the head is well out to avoid a tendency to scrape down the pontoon without getting an offing; such a line is shown in Figure 8(d)3.

The general rule about mainsails is that they are hoisted before casting off if the wind is ahead, but left until there is clear water and a chance to come head to wind if the wind is astern. In all these instances, it is wise to have the engine switched on and running in neutral so that you are in a position to avoid damage to your own craft or others. Nevertheless, it is an advantage to a small crew to have their little ship under sail at the beginning of a passage, and so cut down the amount of foredeck work and sail trimming that would otherwise have to be done in open water.

Sailing off a mooring

A yacht lying on a mooring is subject to the twin influences of wind and tide, and in the waters of northern Europe it is usually the tide that is the more influential of the two. However, it is the wind that makes a boat go, and control from the moment of departure is achieved by canting the head of the yacht (and thus fixing the sail angle in relation to the wind) in a particular direction *before* casting off. Figure 9 gives the essentials of what should be done. The two-man crew have hoisted main and jib while the yacht is still attached to the buoy, and the craft is lying head to wind with sails flapping and the tide coming in on the port bow. The crew decide to use these factors to their advantage to get away on the port tack, and in Figure 9(b) one crew member is 'walking' the warp that formerly held the boat to the buoy aft down the port side of the craft to cant the head to starboard; the other is at the helm, and as the jib fills he brings the sheet in and calls out 'let go!' to his companion on the foredeck. The latter pulls in the mooring rope, coils and stows it; the helmsman hardens in the mainsheet

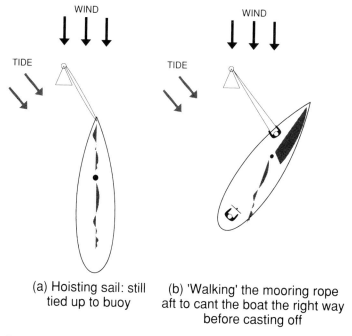

(a) Hoisting sail: still tied up to buoy

(b) 'Walking' the mooring rope aft to cant the boat the right way before casting off

Figure 9 Sailing off a mooring

and the yacht moves off on the port tack well clear of the buoy, helped by the tide.

There are two alternatives, one of them useful when the wind is feeble, the other when it is strong. In calm weather the ship's head may be canted by backing the jib, but the crew must be careful not to drift astern and foul other yachts on adjacent moorings. In strong winds a single crew member may not be able to hold and 'walk' the warp aft alone, and the solution is to run a line from the stern to the ring of the buoy, through it and back again. When the bow warp is slackened, the stern one stays taut and the bows swing away from the buoy to give the right angle for casting off and getting away under sail.

2   Using the engine

Boat salesmen seem to encourage their customers to believe that handling craft under power is just like steering a car – with the difference that some sort of fan down at the back end pushes it along. The real difference is that in a car the engine drives a shaft that turns the back wheels in a fore-and-aft mode, whereas a boat engine drives a propeller that rotates sideways, somewhat in the manner of a screw entering a block of wood. Propellers can be right-handed or left-handed; the right-handed propeller turns clockwise when going ahead and anticlockwise when going astern. Left-handed propellers turn anticlockwise when going ahead and clockwise when going astern. Both types of propeller 'climb' through the water as they turn, and part of the resultant force has a sideways component. This is the 'paddlewheel effect' referred to in Chapter 1; it can be a boon in tight corners and a bane when windage or tide complicates turning manœuvres.

When going ahead from stationary with a right-handed propeller, and no rudder pressure to counteract the thrust of the blades, the bow of the boat will go to port and the stern will swing to starboard. The primary reason for the swing is that the lower blades of the propeller are pushing down into dense water, while the upper blades are moving in less dense water and thus have less effect. Consequently, the first lesson for the shorthanded crew is that making a U-turn ahead from rest under engine should preferably be made to port with a right-handed propeller, and to starboard with a left-handed one.

Going astern

When a boat moves astern from stationary there are a number of modifying factors affecting her progress. Less power is available when going astern because the gearbox gives of its best when in forward drive, and the propeller is also less efficient because it is working, as it were, upside down and back to front. The amount of sideways movement, or torque, is likely to be greater, and the rudder is largely ineffective in the early stages when no sternway has been made. A further point is that at the beginning of a movement astern the rudder has little to do and may as well be kept amidships. These apparently negative factors can, however, be turned to good account by the shorthanded skipper when there is a choice of berths on entering a marina.

It has been pointed out above that with a right-handed propeller the tendency when going ahead is for the bow to go to port and the stern to starboard; the corollary must be that when going astern the bow goes to starboard and the stern to port. With a right-handed propeller the best choice of a berth will always lie on the port side, because the bow can go in to the pontoon at a slight angle as the yacht comes to rest and then, by going astern, the berthing craft will 'walk' back alongside as the reversed screw pulls her in. The second person on board has time to secure the head warp and then move back to take the stern warp from the helmsman. Thus you should go for port side to when the propeller is a right-hander; with a left-handed propeller, the best choice is of course to seek for a berth to starboard.

What the rudder can do

Another way in which the two-man crew can conserve effort and avoid lengthy manœuvring is to find out the size, and then make use of, the yacht's turning circle. The revolutions of the propeller create a vortex of water that is converted to useful forward motion by the rudder, and without the rudder a hull will tend to pivot aimlessly around its centre of lateral resistance (CLR). This is the point along the keel where the boat turns on its axis in response to the rudder. A short keel gives a hull less immersed area at the sharp end, so it will pivot readily and have a small turning circle; a long-keeled yacht will be slower to bring round in a circle, and that circle will be larger.

To find out what the rudder will do it is a good plan to establish the turning circles to port and to starboard on a calm day with little wind. Go ahead at cruising speed on a selected bearing and then put the helm hard over. When the crossed wake shows the circle is complete, motor back over the slick and note the size of the circle by reference to the length of the boat. Usually, the figure arrived at will be just under three times the length of the craft, and that figure in feet or metres can be noted in the log. Its usefulness is that a lightly manned craft may venture more readily into a waterway between pontoons or into a harbour basin in search of a berth for the night when the crew know that a U-turn of so many feet or metres will get them rapidly out of it again. A similar note should be made of the turning circle with opposite rudder; and it is sometimes possible to vary the tightness of the turn by using sails. A partly unrolled headsail may bring the bow round quickly, and a few feet of mizzen at the right moment will do the same for the stern. Precise knowledge of the size of turning circle is a great time saver and enables a small crew to make the kind of positive manœuvre that brings approving nods from bystanders on a quayside or yacht club veranda.

Wind

The best way of finding out the effect of wind on the hull is to go out into open water, put the engine in neutral, take your hands off the wheel or tiller, and see what happens. In most cases, your craft will ease to a stop, pivot on its CLR and fall away with the wind. After that it is most likely to alternate between a stern-on and a beam-on drift downwind as pressure on the furled headsail and mainsail, mast and deckhouse, creates a slow swing between the two headings. The initial yaw away from the wind is the most important movement to record, for it provides a neat no-engine solution to the problem of getting into a downwind berth with narrow margins. In Figure 10(a) a boat has stopped dead in the water at an angle to the wind, and the initial yaw has carried her neatly into the gap, with the two-man crew standing by with warps and boathooks and plenty of fenders on the pontoon side. The alternative method of coming in parallel to the gap, then drifting into it (Figure 10(b)), is less efficient because the yaw carries the stern in first with a bump. Similarly, the zigzag technique tried in Figure 10(c), with the yacht stopping opposite the gap and then going ahead and astern to maintain its parallel

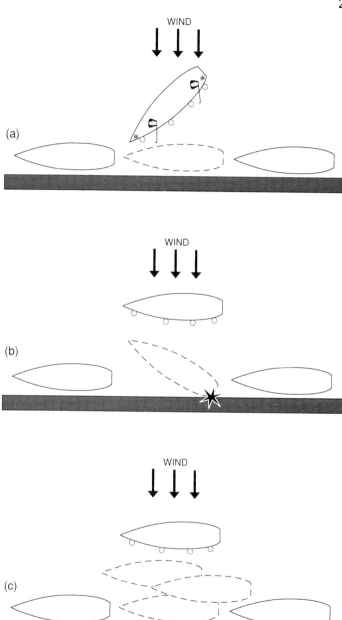

Figure 10 Using the yaw to enter a berth

position as it drifts in, is both less elegant and more alarming to the crews of nearby craft. They are likely to react by emerging with mops and spare fenders to stave off a potential scrape on their topsides.

The tight corner

Knowledge of the boat's behaviour when going ahead and astern, its turning circle and the effect of yaw, will all come into play when the yacht is in a cul-de-sac and is pinned there by wind or tide. A typical instance is outlined in Figure 11. Searching up and down the rows of pontoons for a berth, the boat moves into a particular lane where a vacancy seems promising. As so often in life, the move is one of those triumphs of optimism over experience, and once committed the craft has gone nearly to the sealed end before it is realized that there is not enough room for it at the chosen spot. Knowing the size of the boat's turning circle, the crew at the wheel or tiller sees that a U-turn is not feasible.

Figure 11(a) shows what happens if the usual backing and filling under engine is attempted. Wind pressure on the starboard side of the craft frustrates each successive endeavour to put the boat's head through the eye of the wind, and ground is being steadily lost with each manœuvre. In Figure 11(b) the canny helmsman has appreciated that this is the place to use yaw, port rudder and full astern to get the boat facing into the wind and towards the exit. The four stages in Figure 11(b) show first the boat being brought to a stop at 1, so that the yaw will carry it down to 2. Port rudder is then applied, and the engine put full astern. At 3

Figure 11 Yaw, rudder and full astern to get head to wind

29

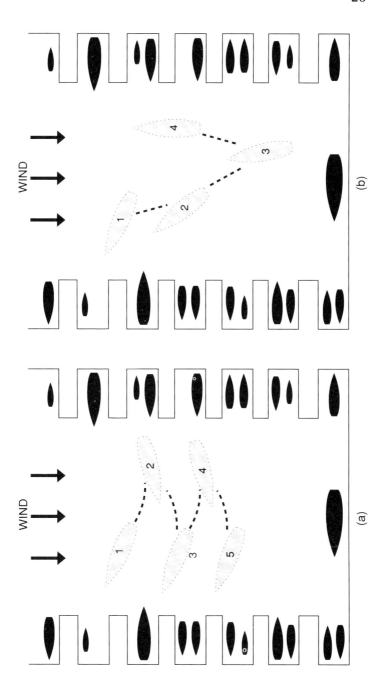

WIND

(b)

WIND

(a)

the rudder is returned amidships and the engine put to half ahead, and at 4 the boat is on its way out to try its luck down another row of berths.

Getting *into* a tight corner may require some lateral thinking on the lines that, although going in bows on is the normal state of affairs, there are occasions when stern first is best. It may happen that the only available berth in a marina is a little wider than the yacht, and has a strong tide *and* wind pouring into the space. It is apparent from the beginning that going in bows first and relying on a burst of reverse to check way is going to fail, so the solution is to use the engine as a braking mechanism for a stern-to entry. The well-fendered yacht – and that means fendered on both sides *and* at the stern – slowly stems wind and tide, using the engine at slow ahead and the rudder to hold it straight and true while natural forces carry it into the berth. This technique will be handy at places where the tide runs through the pontoons, such as Treguier and Gosport, and the cardinal rule of the shorthander – 'slowly does it' – will apply.

Towing

Very little towing takes place under sail nowadays. It is a job for the engine, and we had best start with the commonplace task of towing the dinghy. Rigid tenders are often left in the water during short passages in fine weather, because unless the parent craft is fitted with stern davits there is an understandable reluctance on the part of a two-man crew to haul the dinghy out and secure it. Using a single towrope – often the dinghy painter – the chief requirement is to pay out enough line so that the tender rides on the yacht's sternwave and the bow does not dig into the water, leading to foundering or a capsize.

Inflatables require different handling. They need a stout painter at each end for two reasons. The first is that, as there is more buoyancy and stability at the stern of an inflatable, it is good practice to have a stern line fitted so that the dinghy can be tied or held at both ends, allowing crew to get in and out safely at the widest part. The second reason is that if towing is intended it is sensible to have a very short scope indeed, with the *stern* of the dinghy hauled up on the stern of the towing craft to frustrate flipping and filling. By and large, a small crew would do well to get the inflatable on deck for even the briefest passage, as baling out or recovering one half-filled with water or spray is a considerable task. The best solution is to have it out on deck with the bow chamber deflated so as to save space, yet be readily available for use as a large horseshoe recovery buoy in the event of a man overboard. Inflating one chamber is a small price to pay for avoiding worrying about the rubberized, air-filled, skittish object bouncing along behind.

When asked to take another craft in tow – typically a sailing dinghy that has run out of wind, or a small motorboat that has misjudged its fuel supply – the two essentials are to find the right engine speed and a secure lodging for the towrope at both ends. Again, the golden rule is slowly does it, and a simple signal code should be agreed beforehand between tower and towed: arms outspread, perhaps, with hands down for less speed; hands up and above the shoulders for more; thumbs up when the rope has been made fast; a wave-off gesture to let it go.

Few yachts have really substantial bollards and cleats on the foredeck in the 1990s, and it may be tactful to suggest that the towrope is put round an anchor winch, a through-deck mast, or the forestay fitting. In some cases it can be made into a bridle going right round a wheelhouse or cabin top. Avoid putting the towrope through a sharp-edged fairlead. When being towed, remember to tie down a round-the-mast towrope that will otherwise slide up the mast and pull the boat over.

Chafe is the principal enemy while towing. If it is not possible to encase the rope in strong plastic tubing where it passes over the gunwale, use towels, washing-up cloths, an old sail, or even a sleeping bag, to cut down friction.

Doing a good turn by towing somebody may sometimes bring its own reward. I once pulled a motorboat out of fuel into port to find that the owner was a chandler who had an engine part I had been seeking for many months; he was good enough to lash it to a bottle of champagne and send it down to the harbour. Horror stories are sometimes told about salvage claims, and the legal side of offering or taking a tow is covered in other works dealing with the subject. (See Brian Calwell *Sea Lawyer*, Adlard Coles, 1986; and Conrad Dixon *Grounding, Stranding and Wreck*, Ashford Press Publishing, 1988.) For the most part, offers and acceptances of tows are made in a friendly spirit with no expectation of gain or reward, so there should be no reservations on either side.

The other engine

Engine failure can be a devastating blow to the morale of a small crew – especially when in sight of a safe haven after a long passage. The long-term remedies will be dealt with later in this chapter. What is sketched out here is an emergency procedure useful to lightly manned craft when sanctuary is but a few hundred yards off and the sea relatively calm. The outboard petrol engine normally used to propel the dinghy has low compression, which makes it easy to start. It is the logical back-up to the main engine which, nowadays, tends to be a diesel. Putting the dinghy in the water and trying to tow the parent craft from the bow is likely to be a tedious business, with the line alternatively straightening and dipping in the water and the towed craft swinging about, rather in the manner of a lapdog being pulled along by a dowager from tree to tree in the park. It is much more efficient to lash the dinghy alongside, preferably secured by bow and stern lines and two springs, at either the port or starboard quarter, so that the push of the outboard propeller, and the directional impulse provided by the rudder of the parent craft, are not too far apart. With one crew member in the dinghy tending the throttle and the other steering in the cockpit it is possible to make slow but steady progress to a berth.

Engine care

Diesel engines are relatively idiot-proof, and the steps that must be taken to keep them that way may be put into a single sentence. The essentials are clean, 'solid' fuel, a good spark, plenty of oil, and an effective cooling system. Clean fuel depends on effective filters, and 'solid' fuel means no air locks in the fuel pipes. The battery must deliver amps and watts on demand, and the oil in the sump and gearbox should be changed every fifty hours. Overheating is the commonest problem with diesels, and there are two things to do when the temperature gauge needle goes into the red. First, check the water inlet and clean out its filter. Next, make sure that the belt leading to the water pump is doing its job and then look at the impeller that revolves inside the pump casing. If some of the rubber vanes of the impeller have broken off, the spare impeller should be fitted. A drop in oil pressure may indicate a loss or contamination of sump oil, while a slowdown in both the engine note and the forward speed may be a sign that the gearbox oil is leaking away. Uneven running is a sign of clogged or broken injectors, and it is probably best to keep going at low revs until skilled attention can be given with the boat at rest in harbour.

Non-starting engines

When absolutely nothing happens after going through the starting procedure it is best to begin by checking the electrical contacts, switches and fuses, and then to remove rust from, and smear Vaseline on, the battery terminals. If the starter motor turns but there is no ignition, it may mean that the glow plug part of the preheat system needs replacing or, more likely, that air is not getting in to mix with the fuel because the stop knob or lever is still applied. Or it may be that there is no fuel at all and recourse must be had to the two-gallon emergency container carried as part of the spares.

Uneven running might mean contaminated fuel: it is good practice to bleed the bottom of the tank by opening the drain plug at its base and removing a cupful of fuel, so as to get rid of rust particles and water droplets that collect there. With the engine still running roughly, the next move is to clear the sediment traps, check filters along the fuel route, and turn the bleed screws to squeeze air out of the system. A stuttering engine may provide a clue to its ills through the exhaust smoke. Black smoke is a sign of lack of air or worn injectors: white smoke indicates water in the cylinders and possibly a cracked cylinder head. Blue smoke reveals that oil is burning somewhere, and may point to a leaking head gasket.

Slow turning at the beginning points to a run-down battery, and unless you have a separate starting and domestic battery layout it is essential to be extremely frugal in the consumption of wattage for some time. The prime current-gulpers are refrigerators, VHF radios and radar sets, but even the tricolour light at the masthead will use a great deal of electricity when burning all night. Of course, good manners dictate that you do not run engines for charging purposes in marinas during summer evenings. And it is only proper to turn off the engine when the boat is in a lock, so as to avoid filling the chamber with fumes and giving everybody headaches from the echoing noise the diesel makes in such confined spaces.

Engine spares

Both members of a crew of two need to know how to get the outboard and the main engine going, what the spares are, where they are kept, and how to use them.

In the case of the outboard, the essential spares are sparkplugs, some petrol unmixed with oil, a playing card and a fine needle. Oiling of plugs is a perpetual problem. If a wipe with a cloth does not do the trick, the quickest answer is to put in a new plug. If there is no spare on board, the next move is to take out the old plug and burn off the oil by putting the ignition end of the plug on the lighted gas jet of the galley cooker. There is a desirable side effect on raw, misty days in that a heated plug starts to work much more readily than a cold one. Spare petrol should be carried because oil collects in the crevices and dilution with petrol brings the mixture to the right amalgamation for firing – but great care must be taken that the spare petrol tin is so labelled that it cannot be confused with the diesel containers.

The contact breaker points are often furred up by a combination of salt, oil and dirt, and passing a playing card between them maintains a clean inner surface without doing any damage to the metal. The fine needle is to prick out the tiny airhole in the centre of the filling cap, so that air pressure on the surface of the fuel keeps it flowing to the carburettor. Where an engine starts and then fizzles out after a minute or so the cause is often a blocked ventilation hole.

The spares for a diesel engine need to be more comprehensive, and the list that follows should cover problems short of mechanical malfunction, such as a jammed gearbox or a cracked propshaft:

- Enough oil for complete replenishment of the sump and gearbox should a leak empty both of them.
- Jubilee clips and spare hoses for each size fitted.
- Two gallons of fuel in a secure and well-marked container.

- An impeller for the water pump.
- An oil filter.
- A drive belt for the alternator and another for the water pump.
- A fuel filter and a glass for the water trap.
- Heavy-duty grease for the stern tube and the water pump.

3 Getting ready to sail

Bending on sails

Putting up sails is not at all like fitting curtains or rigging an awning, for sails are designed to convert wind to forward motion and the first care of a small crew is to make sure that the canvas does not supply power before you want it. This usually means keeping the bulk of the sail in the bag until it is attached to something substantial. It should thus be put into the bag so that the right bits come out first. In the case of the mainsail, the clew goes into the bag last and comes out first; with a headsail the tack goes in last and comes out first. When bending on either type of sail the key to safe working is to tie the full sailbag to a grabrail or a foredeck fitting and make one of the sail corners fast before releasing the bulk from the bag. Letting the sailbag blow away after emptying it can also be mildly embarrassing; it should be a matter of strict routine that as one crew member pulls the sail out of the bag the other pops the latter smartly down the forehatch out of the way. Of course, if you have a self-furling jib none of this foredeck work will be necessary, and you can command your jib almost at the flick of a rope.

Two people will be needed to achieve a well-setting mainsail, and the central object is to stretch the foot properly. Once the tack has been shackled or tied to the eye at the inboard end of the boom, one crew member will tug the foot and its associated slides or fastenings as tight as possible while the other threads the outhaul – the piece of cord tied to the clew of the sail – through an eye at the end of the boom, back through the clew eyelet and so on until three or four turns are on, the foot may be hauled taut, and the outhaul knotted to keep it that way. How tight should the foot be? Tight enough for stretch creases to appear parallel to the boom; they will disappear when the sail is hoisted. For safety's sake, the boom must be held reasonably rigid by a tight mainsheet, or secured in a crutch or notch, while both sail benders stand on the windward side of their work to keep clear of the boom jerking about in the breeze.

Shorthanders cannot afford tangles and the double labour of bending on, taking down and rehoisting a sail, so that with a mainsail one crew member is at the halyard while the other is running the luff through his or her fingers to make sure that the slugs or slides are going on the track the right way round. In the case of the foresail, it is wise to make certain that each piston closes properly around the wire stay as these spring-loaded hanks sometimes jam open and subsequently disengage from the forestay at awkward moments. Mizzen and mainsail battens should be numbered, lettered or colour-coded so as not to waste time in matching pockets with battens.

Hoisting sail

A small crew will need to establish an order of work for hoisting sail, and then stick to it. Generally, in a sloop or cutter it is best to start with the mainsail, because with the predominating Bermudan rig this sail can only be put up easily while the boat is head to wind. As this is seldom the direction in which the yacht wants to go, it can be pointed into the wind under engine immediately after casting off while the mainsail goes up, and then it follows its appointed course. In a Bermudan ketch the order is mizzen, jib and mainsail last, because full control will be achieved once the first two sails are up and drawing properly. Gaff ketches and schooners can get under way downwind with a pull on the peak halyards that brings one end of the gaff up with a scrap of mainsail. Yawls have to behave like sloops and start with a mainsail hoist because their mizzens are steering rather than driving sails.

Hoisting the mainsail is not just a matter of hauling away and hoping for the best – that method accounts for the large number of yachts seen lumping along with slack mainsail luffs, wrinkles everywhere and booms drooping at the cockpit end. A well-set main starts with one of the crew taking a pull on the topping lift to get the boom above the horizontal. This takes the strain off the slides and prevents wrinkles forming on the mast side of the mainsail that no amount of subsequent tweaking will eliminate. The same crew member makes the topping lift temporarily fast and transfers his attention to the main halyard.

Modern yachts are fitted with mainsail winches, but the hoister will have more control over the process by pulling down hand-over-hand on the halyard until three-quarters of the mainsail is up. He or she can both feel and see that the halyard is not foul of crosstrees or mast fittings, and be aware of any stickiness on the part of the slides. By transferring the halyard to the drum of the winch and putting three turns around it, the rest of the sail can then be sweated up with either the second crew maintaining the tension at the free end of the halyard or, more usually when at sea, with the solitary foredeck toiler winding the winch with one hand and keeping the free end tight with the other. Once up, the halyard stays on the drum and the free end is cleated and coiled.

More about mainsails

The foregoing applies to orthodox mainsails, but not all are hoisted from the foot of the mast. With the control-lines-aft system the advantages of hoisting the sail from the cockpit are balanced by the disadvantages arising from friction. Keeping the number of blocks to a minimum, avoiding near-right angles for the lines, and putting the ends into compartmented fabric pouches, make life easier – but it is winch work all the way to get the sail up. In the case of the in-mast or behind-mast mainsail reefing systems, there is the same advantage of working from the cockpit end of the boom and bringing the sail out with a block on a traveller, but no battens are possible and a loose-footed mainsail is invariably less efficient than one secured to a boom. How much less efficient? The vertically rolling mainsail tends to be cut flatter and is about 10 per cent smaller in area than standard sails in boats of the same class.

Another type of mainsail is the fully battened variety which outperforms the conventional sort, but has to be stowed with lazyjacks to lie properly on a boom. A crew member has, of course, to go forward in the usual way. There is no ideal mainsail for the shorthanded, but the 'best buy' recommendation must be for the in-mast or behind-mast vertical reefing and setting system, because the loss of drive in fine weather is more than compensated for by the ease of sail reduction in foul. A crew of two that is only occasionally supplemented by friends will be glad of the peace of mind that in-mast or on-mast furling systems can give.

Final touches

The hoister or setter of the mainsail has to make a few final adjustments once the sail is completely up. The downhaul will be loose at this stage, and the tensioning of the luff is accomplished by pulling down and securing the downhaul. The kicking strap must be attached to the boom, and the crew should step back and see that the mainsail is free of wrinkles and pulling well. Putting away the winch handle in its pouch, the crew member can move to the cockpit confident that the mainsail is properly at work and that, having got it right at the beginning, the rest can mostly be done from aft in perfect safety.

Getting the best out of the mainsail

A flat mainsail is sometimes sought by the racing yachtsman in light airs when the headsail is doing most of the work, and it is achieved by being brutal with the main sheet and the kicking strap and, sometimes, hauling the main sheet and blocks up to windward on the traveller so that the boom lies on the centre line of the boat. However, when cruising you will find that mainsails work best with a pronounced curve in the leech and a full belly – the flat mainsail leads to weather helm, excessive heeling and leeway, and less forward progress. A fuller sail profile is achieved when the end of the boom is allowed to rise as the kicking strap is eased, the main sheet slackened, and the main sheet and blocks brought to windward to compensate for the change of the angle of presentation to the wind.

How much curve do you normally need? The best way of finding out the right amount of curve is to squint up the leech from the cockpit and see where the top batten lies in relation to the boom. If it is parallel, that is about right. If the rear of the batten is to leeward of the boom, you need to reduce the curve by tightening the main sheet and kicking strap, and letting the main sheet and blocks move a little to leeward down the traveller. With the rear of the batten pointing to windward it is a question of freeing the kicking strap and sheet, bringing the sheet and blocks a little closer to the wind on the traveller, and looking aloft as you do so to see when the top batten and the boom are parallel again. The leech line is for fine tuning when a flutter develops along the leech which the battens are powerless to correct. Be gentle in using the leech line lest you create a puckering in the cloth that interferes permanently with the flow of air over the trailing edge and ruins the set of the sail altogether.

Hoisting and tuning the headsail

The hoister of a headsail has to bear three things in mind every time he or she goes on the foredeck. The first is that when the sail ties come off they need to be stowed in a pocket, lashed round the waist or thrown down the forehatch to get them out of the way. Second, the sheets must be loose and floppy along the deck to avoid tripping, and on no account should the crew member stand in a bight of rope that is going to tighten as he or she hauls away. Last, the headsail must have 'soft' sheet attachments so that a flogging sail will not brain its handler.

Unlike the mainsail, the headsail should be winched up all the way, and the first step is to wind on at least three turns of the halyard around the headsail winch drum. When the sail is fully hoisted the next step is to cleat and coil the halyard before finding a safe place for the winch handle. Taking it aft to the cockpit is not a good idea as most handles are lost that way. The best solution in a lightly manned yacht is to stow and secure the handle in a mast pouch. The reason for insisting that the winch should be used for the whole of a headsail hoist is so that the crew member is safely installed at one side of the mast most of the time, and will not be dislodged by a flapping headsail.

Modern headsails are designed with camber allowing maximum curvature at a point roughly halfway between luff and leech, and changing the shape and position of the curve improves performance. In light airs it is common practice to slacken the halyard; but as the wind increases the camber of the sail moves aft, and it becomes baggy and unresponsive so that the curve must be restored by hardening up.

Use of telltales

Controlling the foot and luff of a headsail is the function of the sheet, but unscientific adjustments will not help a great deal because it is the position of the sheet blocks rather than the amount of sheet paid out that has the greatest influence on the effectiveness of the headsail. Telltales fitted to headsails will show if the

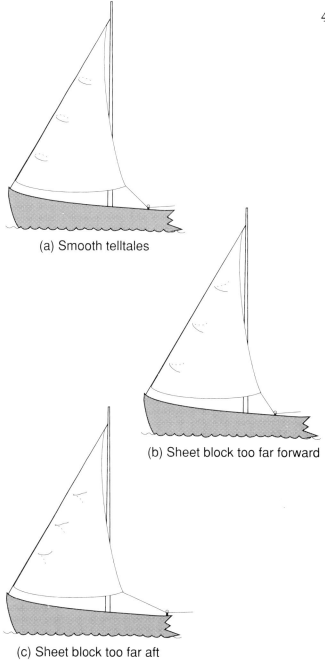

(a) Smooth telltales

(b) Sheet block too far forward

(c) Sheet block too far aft

Figure 12 Headsail sheeting

sheet blocks are in the right place. Known as wools or woolies in Australia and New Zealand, these telltales are mere wisps of natural fibre, brightly coloured and drawn through the sailcloth with a needle. The information they give is best interpreted by the helmsman, who can see them easily, and passed on to the other crew member on the lee sidedeck.

In Figure 12(a) the telltales are flowing slowly and easily. In Figure 12(b), however, the sheet block is too far forward, so that the lower part of the headsail has disturbed and fluttery telltales indicating loss of power at the foot of the sail. (The upper part is functioning well, as the smooth uppermost telltale makes plain.) The crew on the sidedeck should bring the block aft to change the angle of pull of the sheet and thus improve the curvature of the sail. In Figure 12(c) this has been overdone: the block is now too far aft and the lowest telltale shows unmistakable signs of oversheeting, while the uppermost one has wind escaping at the luff. Bringing the block forward again and, perhaps, adjusting sheet tension, will cure the fault. Both crew members should practise reading the telltales; and, when in doubt, it is worth remembering that the set of the headsail is not always apparent from the cockpit, and there is no substitute for going forward and looking at the luff curve, the foot curve and the camber for flat spots. When the yacht is rolling with the run of the waves you will also be able to see where wind is being spilled from the headsail and apply the right remedy in terms of tighter halyard, or a change of lead of the headsail sheet, whether telltales are fitted or not.

The spinnaker

For years the accepted wisdom was that spinnakers were exotic and specialist sails needing five strong men to set and eight to recover them. They were strictly for the racing fraternity. Cruisers did not have the extra halyard, the pole and the fittings needed to set and furl a spinnaker; and the management of sheet and guy, uphaul and downhaul, was deemed to be an elaborate ballet exercise for experts only. A brilliant Swedish invention with the trade name of Spinsafe changed the situation completely; a new technique was devised in which an extending plastic spiral spring encloses the sail when it is being set and recovered. This device can be operated by two people from the cockpit. Figure 13 shows the elements of its operation. A shorthanded crew should rig the spinnaker pole beforehand and shackle the guy and sheet to the tack and clew. The spinnaker is hoisted within the spiral, and the slow withdrawal of the latter gives a reefed sail if you want it that way. A downhaul makes furling easy, and the furled spinnaker is either left where it is in light weather or carried outside the shrouds and crosstrees aft for putting away or further use.

The purpose of this latter exercise is twofold. Short-handers often use the sidedeck as working space, because it is one of the few areas on board where a pulling and separating pressure can be applied to gear, and it can be a useful dodge when cruisers are racing under handicap. A two-handed crew with a 'made-up' spinnaker hidden from the view of opponents has a considerable surprise weapon up its sleeve when the wind comes free.

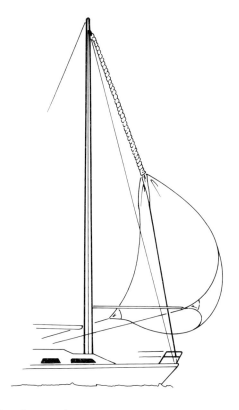

Figure 13 Spinsafe at work

Care of sails

When handling sails always look for signs of loose or broken stitching, particularly around the batten pockets and the eyelets at the foot of the mainsail. Minor running repairs are well within the capacity of a small crew, and the two most useful types of stitching are described in the next paragraph. Should you be unfortunate enough to get a big rip in a sail, it is best to make emergency repairs with adhesive tape and leave the clever stuff to the professional sailmaker. Probably the most destructive thing you can do is to put a sail away wet; headsails, in particular, will need to be taken out of the bag on arrival in port and then hoisted to flap dry. Similarly, a wet mainsail left hanked to a boom must be hoisted to dry before the covers go on since mildew, once it has a good grip, is difficult to get rid of and the smell will linger on in the sailcloth when the fungus itself is no longer visible.

Sail repairs

Sails tend either to come apart at the seams or to be ripped by contact with something sharp. In the former case, the repairer mimics the stitches made by the manufacturing machine, using the original holes and then making a zigzag pattern by sewing first one way and then the other, as depicted in Figure 14(a). Rips and tears are dealt with as in Figure 14(b), where herringbone stitches close up the edges – but do not create wrinkles by overlapping the cloths in any way. The key to success is not to pull the stitches too tight. If you need a permanent repair, then cover the stitched cut on both sides with a patent sail-repair tape that is adhesive on one side.

Stowage

The stowage of bagged sails in a small boat is a problem worthy of the skills of a Houdini, and the commonest solution is to put them in cockpit lockers or the forecabin. The difficulty with cockpit lockers is

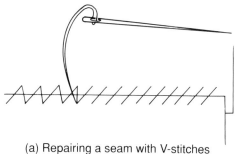

(a) Repairing a seam with V-stitches

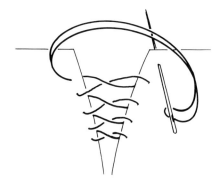

(b) Repairing a rip with herringbone stitches

Figure 14 Sewing repairs

that they may have a 'cuckoo in the nest' in the shape of a bagged inflatable dinghy, and mooring warps, bathing ladders, fenders and boathooks tend to congregate in the same spot. One sail only per locker is generally the best rule because of the problem of getting at a second when you want it badly. If you have a storm jib stowed beneath a large genoa, it is odds on that the former will be needed just at the time when the latter is hopelessly jammed in the keyhole. But with one sail per locker, the question is what to do with the rest.

The shorthanded crew always has the advantage of extra living space so that fo'c'sle stowage is a realistic option. There are only four points to bear in mind. The bags must be slim enough to go through the forehatch. They should be stowed on the bunks athwartships so that they do not roll off, and the titles on the bags must be easily read. Finally, treat them as you would injured or seasick crew. Secure them in place with the leecloths so that they will not leap about and fall on the crew member who comes to bear them away to do their duty.

4   Manœuvring under sail

Points of sailing

Everyone loves a soldier's wind with the sails at right angles to the breeze and filling like the canvas in an old Dutch oil painting, but it is more usual to have to point the yacht's head in several directions during a day's cruise. The range of headings is set out in Figure 15 so that you may reconcile the terms with the angle of the fore-and-aft line to the wind. At the top of Figure 15 is the hopeless condition that sometimes arises when a tack is misjudged and the boat ends up head to wind with sails flapping uselessly. The cure is for one of the crew to go forward, seize the clew of the headsail and hold it out so that the wind stills its thrashing. The yacht's head will pay off the other way, so if the headsail is held out to starboard the bow will cant to port and the mainsail will begin to fill and give thrust. When the headsail is released the yacht will take up first the steering shy position, and then broaden off to close-hauled.

Steering shy is a state normally arrived at deliberately from close-hauled in order to make sail changes. It is achieved by sheeting as for close-hauled then steering closer to the wind so that the sails flutter, the speed drops to a couple of knots, and a reef or sail change may

Figure 15 Points of sailing

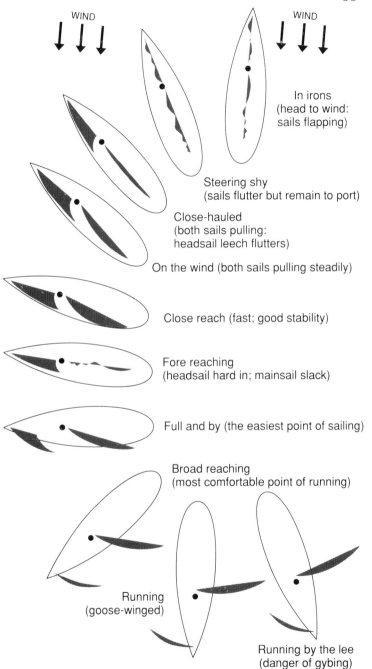

WIND

WIND

In irons
(head to wind:
sails flapping)

Steering shy
(sails flutter but remain to port)

Close-hauled
(both sails pulling:
headsail leech flutters)

On the wind (both sails pulling steadily)

Close reach (fast; good stability)

Fore reaching
(headsail hard in; mainsail slack)

Full and by (the easiest point of sailing)

Broad reaching
(most comfortable point of running)

Running
(goose-winged)

Running by the lee
(danger of gybing)

be made. It has the advantage that no ground is lost to leeward, and the motor is often started to help hold the boat in position. The close-hauled mode is where the craft is steered as close to the wind as possible with taut sheets to make progress to windward; it is what racing craft are specifically designed to do well. The helmsman watches the leech of the headsail closely to keep it just a-shiver and make good headway. However, this is not necessarily the fastest method of making ground against the wind, as Figure 16 will demonstrate.

In Figure 16 a gentle wind will give a speed of 3 knots to a close-hauled yacht, 4 knots to one on the wind and at a 55° angle to it, and five knots to a yacht on a close reach and at a 60° angle. After one hour on the port tack all three yachts go about and at the end of the second hour you can see that the yacht on the wind is ahead of both the close-reach and the close-hauled ones. Free sheets and a generous attack angle to the wind will often pay better than pinching up and slowing down, or going off so broadly that the extra distance to be covered is not compensated for by additional speed.

Fore-reaching is a way of slowing down to await dawn, or enough water over a bar, without changing direction significantly. It is achieved by hardening in both foresheets and letting the main and rudder look after themselves. Full and by is the easiest point of sailing and broad-reaching gives good speeds down and across a favourable wind, although it is often accompanied by a combination of pitching and rolling that tests sensitive stomachs. Running is a nervous business because the helmsman always fears an uncontrolled gybe with each slight wind shift; and running by the

Figure 16 On the wind beats close-hauled

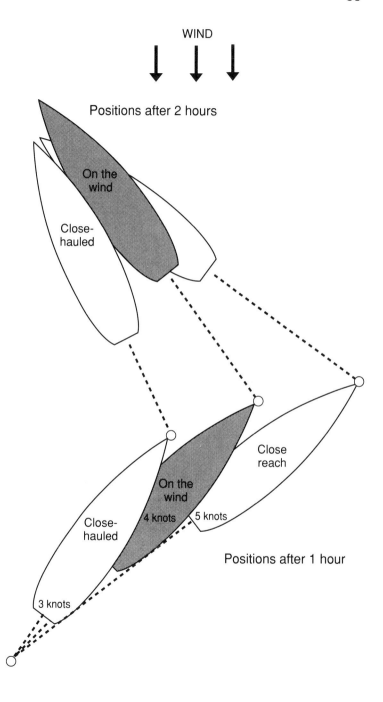

WIND

Positions after 2 hours

On the wind

Close-hauled

Close reach

On the wind

Close-hauled

4 knots

5 knots

3 knots

Positions after 1 hour

lee is positively hair-raising as a sudden gybe will fling the boom across, puts strain on the mainsheet and may damage gear. As depicted in the bottom part of Figure 15, the headsail is masked by the mainsail when running and will flutter uselessly unless one of the crew casts off the 'old' sheet and makes fast the 'new' so that the sails are goose-winged.

A controlled gybe may be accomplished from the cockpit, with the crew member bringing in the mainsail to get the boom safely amidships as the helmsman moves the wheel or tiller to bring the wind on the other side of the mainsail. The boom will go across to the other side with a jerk, but it has a small scope, and with the wind pressing steadily on the mainsail the sheet is let out again to provide maximum thrust.

Working sheets and winches

The headsail sheets are generally led back through blocks or a movable car on a short rail to the winches, and then, if the winches are not of the self-tailing variety, to a cleat. Winches should be fitted 'paired' as in Figure 17(a), so that the sheet is always put on from the outside; this can cause confusion where one crew member handles both winches and sheets. Most people get it right on the starboard side but tend to have trouble with the port winch – because it seems natural to make an identical winding-on movement, which puts the sheets on the inside of the barrel. Worse, once you start that way and put the turns on, it takes time to realize that the winch barrel is not going to rotate as expected and the whole sheet has to come off for a fresh start.

The other great winch problem is when you get a

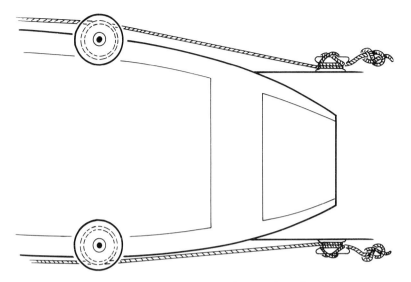

(a) Sheets go on to winches from outboard

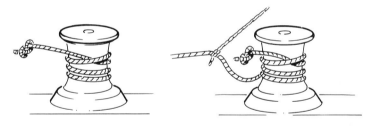

(b) Taking out a riding turn

Figure 17 Winches

riding turn on the barrel so that the sheet is jammed. The only sensible thing to do is to take the strain with another length of rope while the riding turn is taken off, as shown in Figure 17(b). Do *not* poke your fingers under the turns until the strain is off and, if necessary, get your companion to keep a steady pull on the retaining cord as the tangle is sorted out. Where headsail or mainsail sheets run aft to the cockpit and are secured by jam cleats, the shorthanded crew will need extra attachments. Do not trust a jam cleat to hold in winds over Force 5; but secure sheets in addition to an orthodox cleat or to some substantial fitting in the cockpit. Naturally, a small crew will have had the foresight to put figure-of-eight knots on the ends of all the sheets to prevent them pulling through the blocks and being blown overboard at the behest of flailing sails.

Tacking with two

Going about in a sloop, cutter or ketch can be relatively simple because there is usually no work to do with the mainsail and all efforts are concentrated on the headsail. It is also one of those few occasions when formal orders are given by the person at the helm. The process starts with the helmsman steering off a little to maintain speed, then warning the other crew member by saying 'Ready about?'. This tells the crew to get ready to cast the sheet of the leeward drum, but do nothing more until the second order is received.

When the helmsman has reached an advantageous position, a 'smooth' or flat piece of sea between wave clusters, and has the boat going at its best speed, he calls 'Lee oh!' and either pushes the tiller right down, or pulls the wheel hard round so that the bow will swing through the eye of the wind. At this second command the sheet handler lets go the sheet from the lee winch and, if the wind is light, will twirl the coils up off the drum of the winch so that the sheet will have less friction and more pull through the block. The helmsman keeps the rudder hard over and the crewman goes to the other side of the cockpit and makes sure the sheet is ready round the barrel of the windward winch. *He or she does not pull yet.* The thrashing headsail keeps moving, passing through the 'in irons' position shown in Figure 15. A pull too soon at this stage may put even air pressure on both sides of the sails and perpetuate the 'in irons' position; a pull too late and the sheet will foul the shrouds and necessitate the use of the winch handle to get it in. The skilled shorthanded seaman hauls on the sheet at the point when the wind is about 10° on the right side of the bow and has the sheet tight and cleated *before* the weight of the wind comes into the headsail.

Steering

Self-steering gear works best when you are motoring, motor-sailing in light airs or sailing close-hauled, and a small crew should make maximum use of this mechanical aid because it enables a two-person team to keep a better lookout, navigate with greater precision and have longer endurance. In the author's boat, *Waveney Harrier*, the self-steerer is commonly employed when the wind is less than Force 4 and the boat is clear of the land, but never in restricted waters or when a lot of other craft are about. Self-steerers are good but limited servants, and as the wind rises they become less and less responsive until, in a lumpy sea, their reactions are progressively delayed so that the boat starts making an S-shaped course only roughly approximating to the proper heading. Indeed, if you do not switch them off and revert to hand steering they will go in tight circles until relieved of their task.

The autopilot has the advantage over the self-steerer that it will interface with other instruments. Typically, it will follow a shift in wind direction indicated by a windvane, be linked to a fluxgate compass, and have off-course and depth alarms. For shorthanders, there is an autotack attachment so that both crew members can concentrate on handling the sheets; and in thick weather some autopilots will interface with Decca or Loran receivers so that course adjustments are made automatically. However, as with self-steerers, wind and wave forces will make for variations in the course steered, whatever the manufacturer's blurb may say, and there comes a time when the machine has to be switched off. Similar claims are made that response buttons permit yachts to stay on autopilot while in narrow channels or near other yachts, but I would suggest that shorthanders should revert to hand-steering and keep a good lookout rather than put their trust in electronic aids in close-quarters situations.

On a downwind heading it may sometimes be necessary to steer an S-shaped course to get safely over wave ridges, such as those that build up on the Flemish banks or the western approaches to the English Channel. In Figure 18(a) the mean course is a broad reach, but the experienced helmsman is putting the yacht through the crest at an angle of almost 180° to the wind. The triple purpose of the manoeuvre is to maintain steerage way and full control through the crests, lessen the likelihood of water coming aboard, and avoid a broach with the boat falling sideways on the far side of the wave and wallowing helplessly in the trough after it. Once the crest has been passed, the broad reach may be resumed.

Another big problem when steering downwind is that pressure on the sails reduces in the troughs, so

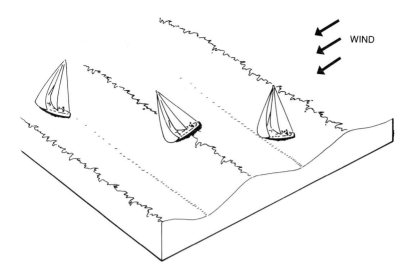

(a) Squaring up on the crest

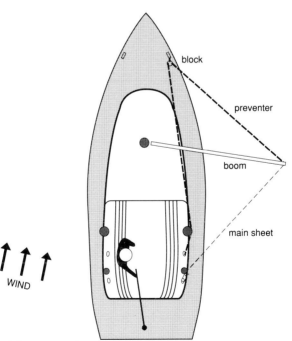

(b) Use of the preventer

Figure 18 Steering downwind

that the boom first gybes across and then gybes again as the quartering wind refills the sails. The cure is to fit a simple device with a number of names. The Americans call it a foreguy; the German term translates as 'boom brake'; and the British refer to a preventer. Essentially it is a piece of rope that controls the sternward movement of the boom in the same way as the mainsheet controls its forward movement. Figure 18(b) shows a preventer in action. It is often contrived from one of the long mooring warps fixed to the boom and carried through a block on the foredeck, or attached to the foot of a shroud, and brought to the cockpit. In Figure 18(b) the mainsheet provides the third side of the triangle and acts in an equal and opposite manner to hold the boom reasonably rigid. The two essentials to bear in mind when rigging a preventer are: one end should be made fast to the extreme end of the boom to exert maximum leverage; the other should not be made up so securely that it cannot be cast off in a second if a change of course is needed. Finally, there is a tendency to forget all about a preventer after it has been in action for an hour or two, and this can lead to red faces when the crew tries to manoeuvre the craft with the boom still firmly pinned both ways.

One last point about steering: it is useless in a sailing boat to try to steer precisely to a degree; far better to steer a mean course with, say, a variation of about 5° each side of the given course. Crew endurance will also be extended if frequent changes are made at the helm. A helmsman is at his best some ten minutes after taking over; after an hour the concentration fades and relief becomes a necessity.

Heaving-to

This most useful manœuvre fits in splendidly with the needs of a small crew, for the ability to stop in open water and get something done with the boat on a relatively even keel is much to be prized. Typically, a lightly manned yacht may want to stop for breakfast after a night at sea, or halt to reduce or increase sail. The simplest technique is to get the boat sailing along close-hauled and then put her about in the manner described earlier in this chapter, *but without touching the sheets at all*. The backed headsail will try to push the bows to leeward; and the tiller, also to leeward and sometimes lashed in that position, tends to hold the bows up to windward. The third component is the mainsail, which gives a little forward motion. The result is a seesawing movement with the boat moving forward, then falling back, then moving forward again. The broad drift downwind and slightly ahead creates a slick of smoothed water that softens the wind-driven waves marching up on the starboard side of the yacht. The hull will heel to the push of the wind, but this can be turned to advantage. If you are heaving-to for a meal it is advantageous – with the galley on the port side of the cabin, as is often the case – to do so on the starboard tack and have the benefits of cooking or making a drink 'downhill' rather than 'uphill'.

Craft with a long keel and a deep forefoot heave-to best of all, and with some modern cruisers and racers of the fin-and-skeg variety it will be necessary to juggle with the sheets to get the best balance. Slackening the mainsail is often helpful, and the headsail sheet may have to be eased to get a pronounced 'bag' of sail between forestay and shrouds.

A yacht retains freedom of action when hove-to,

being able to get under way almost at once by casting off one headsail sheet and hauling tight on the other. One last word of warning: despite appearances, hove-to yachts are probably making a knot, or even two, downwind, and the tactic should never be employed – even in the lightest weather – when the intention is for the crew to have a swim in the open sea.

5   On passage

The passage plan

The elements of a successful passage plan are briefly
outlined here. You have to work out the tides, and
that means taking advantage of every scrap of fair tide
that is on offer. You have to listen to the forecast and
determine what sail shall be carried, erring on the
cautious side in the instance of a small crew. Note
the whereabouts of safe boltholes on the way, and
have alternatives up your sleeve if things go better, or
worse, and the ultimate destination has to be changed.
Select a chart that has the beginning and the end of the
voyage on it and enter the dead reckoning positions for
each hour. If you have an electronic navigation system
this is the time to work out the waypoints, get your
companion to check them, and then key in *and* put
them on the chart.

Write out a list of the buoys, conspicuous land-
marks and lights the night before, and add the useful
D/F stations for the sea area to be traversed. Note
down the frequency and the call signs. For example,
if you are going to be sailing in the western English
Channel the collective frequency is 298.8 kHz and the
dominant station is Start Point with the call sign SP
(··· ·− −·). If this seems like over-preparedness remember that shorthanders have little time to refer to books
on passage. Where a longish passage is contemplated

it is better to arrange things so that the yacht arrives off a strange shore a little before dawn and you get the benefit of a fix from shore lights, and then have all day to get into port. Aim a little upwind or uptide on such occasions so that there is a margin of easy sailing in hand. Eat well before starting, and prepare a hot, soupy stew for storage in a metal vacuum flask in case sea conditions are such that making a meal or hot drink is an ordeal. An hour's nap before getting ready to sail can never be a bad thing.

Avoiding action

Yachts sailing in home waters are not likely to be menaced by rogue whales, or supertankers speeding across the ocean on autopilot with only the ship's dog on the bridge, so when drawing up a realistic list of potential collision risks we would do best to start at the low end of things; with the trivial rather than the dramatic. Commercial fishermen lay out lines of lobster and crab pots marked at each end by flagged buoys and pick-up floats, and this type of gear is not particularly dangerous to passing craft, provided a good clearance of, say, 30 feet or a boat's length is given. There is greater peril from the amateur fisher who sets his pots near a port entrance, and uses an upside-down disinfectant bottle and a trailing grass warp for marking and recovery.

On encountering this kind of fishing gear the crew member on lookout has to have eyes in the back of his head, combining the normal sweep round the forward horizon with a glance backward at pots just passed. If a float begins to follow in the wake, this is a sign that you have picked up something: you will have to go into neutral and search out the old breadknife kept handy for dealing with this problem. Floating nets may be encountered in the summer months off the coast. Drift nets may extend up to two miles from fishing craft, and seine nets can cover a square mile. The worst area in western Europe seems to be the patch of sea between the Riviera and Corsica, where tunny fishermen congregate in great numbers in August and block miles of sea with lines of nets. Merchant ships steam through these lines if they cannot get past them; but yachtsmen should stop and wait, or even turn round to avoid being boarded by excitable individuals demanding enormous sums in damages. In short, if you come across an area of floating nets anywhere it is wise to make a wide detour.

Another warning sign is two fishing boats travelling in parallel as it is likely that they are pair-trawling, or using a Larsen trawl, and have wires slung between them. Consequently, steer round pairs of fishing vessels. Single trawlers with the gear down have wires running at a shallow depth angle from the stern: the only safe thing to do is to pass astern of the bobbing cod-end buoy marking the extremity of the net.

Two-man crews are often reduced to one at night or during long afternoons when the companion is resting. The crew on watch cannot leave his post to check on the more unusual lights and shapes associated with fishing vessels, but must instead know them by heart. The first problem is when is a fisherman fishing? By day, when he has a basket or two cones point to point hoisted up on the forestay. By night he shows green-over-white or red-over-white lights at the masthead, plus the usual navigation lights. The green-over-white combination indicates a trawler; but when shooting the net this changes to two white vertical lights and to a white over a red light when hauling. A red light over a white one is a sign of other types of fishing craft; but purse seiners with an enormous baggy net, which is pulled round in complete circles, show two yellow vertical lights that flash alternately, somewhat in the manner of the lights on motorway maintenance vehicles. Similar avoiding action will be required when approaching dredgers, pipe and cable layers, and clusters of diving boats showing the characteristic blue and white swallow-tailed flags of their trade.

Pair trawlers often train a searchlight on each other when fishing, and then flick the beam in the direction of the lie of the net to show where it is. Fishermen are great gossips and love a chat with passing craft to break the monotony of the day. They will advise about nets, dan buoys and other obstacles in the water, so that a small crew should keep the VHF on when near a fishing fleet to get early notice of dangers on their intended course. Such traffic must of course be confined to the intership channels to keep the distress, urgency and calling channel clear.

Signals and the handling of a yacht on passage

I do not propose to quote chunks of the Collision Regulations to cover all the eventualities a shorthanded crew might encounter on a typical day passage, so what follows is a résumé of the most important obligations. On leaving the quay or marina for the open sea the yacht should keep to starboard in the channel, and at a bend where it is not possible to see anything coming the other way it should sound a prolonged blast of four to six seconds' duration. (In the case of yachts, which are rarely fitted with whistles or sirens, the blast is made with a hand-held foghorn fitted with a replaceable pressure canister and operated by the second member of the crew, who is standing lookout.) In open water with sails up and the engine still running you must hoist a black cone, point upwards, to show that you are motor sailing. Approaching and passing a slow-moving yacht on the same course makes you an overtaking vessel, and you *must* keep clear. In restricted visibility, and still under engine, the requirement is to give a prolonged blast at least every two minutes, but if the engine is off and you are under sail alone the proper sound signal in fog, mist or rain is one prolonged and two short blasts every two minutes. This signal is the letter 'D' in Morse, and the full meaning is 'Keep clear of me; I am manœuvring with difficulty.' If radar is fitted, the set should be switched on and monitored regularly by the helmsman.

A sailing vessel has theoretical precedence over powered craft, except when the latter are constrained by their draught, but the practical interpretation of the rules is that most of the time the little'un keeps out of the way of the big boats, and makes his alterations of course early and obvious. In particular, shorthanded crews have to react very quickly to the six potentially dangerous situations set out in Figure 19.

Let us start with Figure 19(a) where a yacht and a merchantman are on a converging course. The crew member on lookout has been taking the bearing of the ship and notes that the angle hardly changes as they close. There is a risk of collision, and the helmsman will alter course to get round the stern of the ship. In Figure 19(b) two close-hauled yachts are converging, and the rule is that the one on the starboard tack – at the right of the illustration – has the right of way and stands on; the other yacht gives way. In Figure

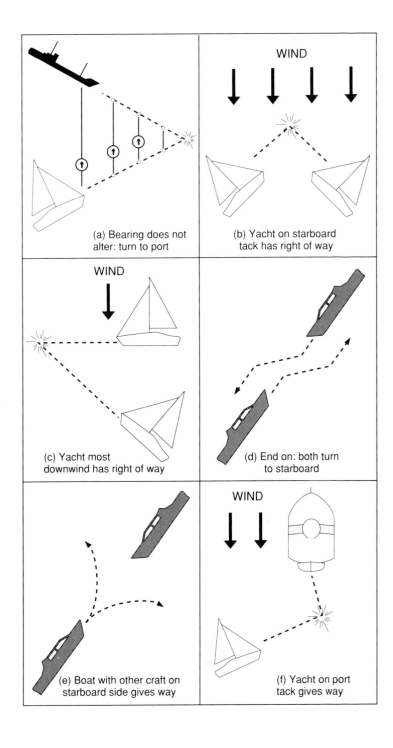

(a) Bearing does not alter: turn to port

(b) Yacht on starboard tack has right of way

(c) Yacht most downwind has right of way

(d) End on: both turn to starboard

(e) Boat with other craft on starboard side gives way

(f) Yacht on port tack gives way

WIND

19(c) both boats are on the same tack and converging; it is the one further from the wind that has the right of way, and the other must yield pride of place. With two craft heading directly for one another, as in Figure 19(d), the rule is that *both* turn to starboard and pass each other port side to port side. Much more common is the state of affairs in Figure 19(e) where two craft are not quite end on to each other, and here the one that has the other on its starboard side gives way. I have shown two alternatives here, but the turn to starboard is more sensible because it achieves the proper passing position shown in Figure 19(d). Finally, we have the 'don't know' problem where the close-hauled yacht at the bottom of the illustration – 19(f) – is confronted by one flying a spinnaker, which hides the mainsail so that there is no knowing whether it is on port or starboard tack. The helmsman of the lightly manned yacht *knows* that he has the wind on his port bow and should give way to the spinnaker-wearing yacht if it is on the starboard tack. He, very sensibly, assumes that this is the case and gives way. Of course, if the close-hauled yacht was on the starboard tack and coming up from bottom right in Figure 19(f), he might behave as though the answer lay with the solution in either 19(b) or 19(c) and stand on: 'might' because there is one more factor to bear in mind. There is a general requirement for craft to keep out of the way of yachts that are racing, and if that was the case the close-hauled boat would get out of the way of the spinnaker flyer whatever tack the former was on.

Figure 19 Rule of the road

Steering and sailing rules at night

A crew of two can make life much more tolerable at night by following three simple rules. A deck-scraping genoa restricts forward visibility, and a headsail with a high-cut foot is infinitely preferable. Spreader lights and strong domestic lighting destroy night vision, and a dim torch will often suffice. Binoculars have a light-gathering function apart from their magnifying properties, and will greatly assist in identifying buoys, ships and shoremarks.

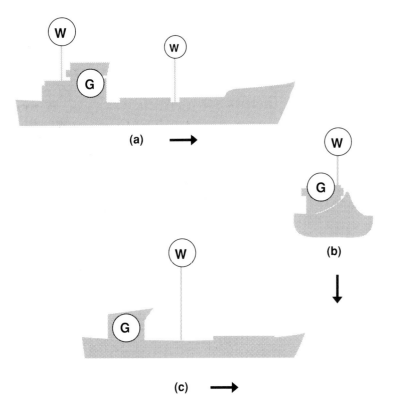

Figure 20 Headings

The track of large vessels under way at night is relatively easy to determine because their two masthead lights give a heading, as shown in Figure 20(a). A ship that is less than 50 metres in length may have a single masthead light, and that makes the divining of its intentions more difficult because the angle of heading has to be reckoned from a comparison of the masthead light with the sidelights. In Figure 20(a) the two-masted ship is passing safely ahead, but in Figure 20(b) and (c), the single white and green lights have the two interpretations shown. In Figure 20(b) the craft is going to pass very close indeed; in Figure 20(c) it is well clear. The proper decision would be to accept the least favourable approach angle and act accordingly. This means slow down, stop or – as in this case – turn to port so that the old adage 'green to green, red to red; perfect safety, go ahead' meets the situation.

Sometimes, the red and green sidelights of an approaching ship seem to come on unrelentingly and there is a panic feeling that he has not seen you. In many cases the merchant ship has you on radar and is going to swing round your stern, but what if it looks as though he does not know you are there? The shorthanded yacht is not in a position to make rapid sail changes or speed off to one side or the other and, indeed, may be prohibited by the collision regulations from doing so. The thing to do is to proclaim your presence. A torch flashed on the sails, a call on the VHF or a white flare will probably do the trick. But if that fails then an undignified U-turn under full power and a dash for one side or the other may be the only answer.

The crossing of separation lanes requires a special technique from the two-person crew because, since these lanes must be crossed at a right angle, or something close to it, the range of action is limited to speeding up, slowing down, turning in the direction of the lane or stopping. The crew member with the hand-bearing compass will be extremely busy on these occasions, as he or she will be taking and calling out the bearings of more than one ship and commenting on the brightness of the lights themselves. A typical commentary might go: 'The tanker to starboard now bears 030° and should cross ahead. Her lights are much brighter. The container ship to port is now showing only her stern light and is going away fast. The yacht behind us is getting closer as I can now see her sidelights plainly. She seems to be on the same course as ourselves, but is about a knot faster. The next one after the tanker to starboard is very dimly lit; I can only see the steaming lights: she bears 065° and looks to be three miles away.' With this kind of information to hand the helmsman makes up his mind; he will pass behind the tanker, aim to get ahead of the next one coming up on the starboard side and speed up to increase his distance from the yacht moving up astern.

Watches

Division of the day at sea into working and resting periods has to take a specific shape when there are only two persons on board to share the load. In order to arrive at the right formulas it is best to start with the traditional six four-hour watch system and then make modifications. For many centuries the pattern of watchkeeping has been:

Hours	Name
2000 to midnight	First watch
midnight to 0400	Middle watch
0400 to 0800	Morning watch
0800 to noon	Forenoon watch
noon to 1600	Afternoon watch
1600 to 2000	Evening watch

In years gone by the evening watch was split into two two-hour periods called the first and second dog watches. This practice is worth retaining because it is the social time of day when few voyagers will want to sleep so that, if the self-steering gear is taking the strain and there is little traffic about, the couple will be able to hold conversations on non-nautical topics, get in a game of Scrabble, or have what the Americans call the happy hour with the daily (small) ration of alcohol.

A practical watchkeeping system must include time enough for a good sleep, but not be so long that the working member becomes too tired to be effective. Four hours on watch at night can be a wearying experience, with the on-watch half of the crew unable to sing, play the radio or clatter around for fear of disturbing the sleeping partner; and that partner is unlikely to get the full spell of allotted rest either. With deductions for partly undressing, getting off to sleep, waking early to worry about strange noises, the heel and motion of the little ship, and wind and weather changes, it is much more likely that the total time slept will only be about two and a half hours out of four. On a passage occupying a single night the watch pattern should be modified to divide the twilight/dark zone into four three-hour periods, giving a twenty-four hour total of eight watches instead of six. Each crew member should, if all goes well and there are no emergencies or traffic lanes to cross, get two two-hour sleeps between 2000 and 0800. The table of hours would be as follows:

Eight watches for a one-night crossing

Hours	*Name*
2000 to 2300	First watch
2300 to 0200	Midnight watch
0200 to 0500	Graveyard watch
0500 to 0800	Morning watch
0800 to noon	Forenoon watch
noon to 1600	Afternoon watch
1600 to 1800	First dog watch
1800 to 2000	Second dog watch

With a two-night passage, as when going to Norway or from southern England round or inside Ushant to the Bay of Biscay, it is best to stick to the traditional system with slight modification for the night hours. On the second night, in particular, the need for a longer rest period is strong and account must be taken of the long twilight in northern latitudes. The seven-watch system below has a third dog watch between 2000 and 2200 and two five-hour watches in the dark hours so that both crew get one long sleep each and, on alternate days, stand only three watches totalling eleven hours. The rota looks something like this:

Seven watches for a two-night passage

Hours	*Name*
2000 to 2200	Third dog watch
2200 to 0300	Midnight watch

0300 to 0800	Morning watch
0800 to noon	Forenoon watch
noon to 1600	Afternoon watch
1600 to 1800	First dog watch
1800 to 2000	Second dog watch

The success of any watch system rests on its immediate implementation once the land drops astern, with crew being disciplined enough to go below to rest even though the sun is shining. Naturally, a sail change or crossing a traffic lane will interfere with the best-laid plans, but the partner sleeping below is like a battery on charge, ready for the new demand on strength and brainpower.

The quality of rest is vital. With only two on board the best (midships) bunks in the boat should be used. The off-watch crew can get into a double, zipped sleeping bag to cut out that squeezed-in feeling that a single bag often conveys. The bunk itself should be habitable on either tack with a full-length leecloth holding the occupant firmly in place. If bad weather threatens, it is important that a couple of spare sleeping bags, well-wrapped in bin liners and stored in a dry locker, are to hand. Nothing damages morale so much as the unalluring prospect of slithering into a damp bag after a spell on the tiller or wheel. The courtesies of a handover should not be neglected. A hot drink brought to the bunkside by the on-watch person when calling his relief; the five minutes spent in the cockpit while the new watchkeeper adjusts to the heave of the sea and gets his eyes settled to the current visibility; the pointing out of ships and shoremarks already identified, before going below to write up the log, take off outer clothing and seek the warm oblivion of the sleeping bag and the sensuous comfort of just being out of the wind for a few hours.

Moving about

Safety starts in the mind, not in the wallet. Careful, controlled movement from handhold to handhold is the key to an injury-free passage, together with putting on the safety harness down below and making sure the fit is right. Always take hold of the grabhandles on leaving the companionway and thereafter transfer one hand at a time to the cockpit coaming, the grabrail on the coachroof, the inner shrouds and the mast itself. Wedge a shoulder or hook an elbow round a stay or taut halyard and, when in the foredeck triangle, brace your feet against cleats, the winch or a hatch to hold position. Crouch, kneel or sit to keep the body weight low, and do not be ashamed to crawl when bringing a sailbag along the side deck – and always on the windward side. Clip on to the jackstay (a safety wire running fore and aft along the deck) as you go in preference to the guardrails, which may not be wholly safe.

In rough weather, when coming out into the cockpit, ask your companion to secure the carbine clip of your safety harness to a padeye *before* you lift yourself out and over the sill. You should use the type of safety harness that has *two* clips on one line. That way you can use the shorter length of line to brace yourself during a sail change or while steering, and the longer one while moving about or working at the foot of the mast. Double-clipping, with that part of the rope between the clips across the body, will hold a dozing crewman, reluctant to go below, firmly in the corner of the cockpit and prevent him being jerked overboard by the pitch and heave of the sea.

Man overboard

Most rescue methods are based on having a crew of several people with, for example, one person steering, one pointing to where the casualty was last seen, another throwing floating objects over the side, and a fourth lowering sails. With just one person on board and one in the water you have to think somewhat laterally. The first necessity is to have a device to haul a heavy, wet, and nine-tenths submerged and perhaps unconscious crew member a couple of feet on to a side deck. No one individual, however strong, will be able to do this unaided. The solution is to carry a lifesling, which is a combined buoyancy aid and hoisting sling that the person in the water can get into, or have it shrugged around him, prior to being lifted out. The recovery procedure is a two-part operation: getting back to the casualty and attaching him to the boat; then pulling him out of the water.

Man overboard always happens without warning. To help you get the drill right every time there is a helpful mnemonic: TESSIE O'SHEA IS LOOKING FOR LIKELY LADS. This stands for TURN, SHOUT, LOOK, LIFESLING and LEE SIDE. Figure 21(a) may make things clearer. The yacht has been going along steadily on the starboard tack when a crew member falls overboard, fortunately observed by his companion. The latter knows that the basis of a recovery is the 'quick-stop' method, with the boat coming head to wind and slowing right down, so he immediately puts the helm down to achieve the hove-to position at A, and as the boat TURNS he SHOUTS to tell the friend in the water that the rescue has started. As the yacht circles back to the 'man overboard' position, the helmsman keeps LOOKING to see where the person in the water is in relation to the turning yacht. When between points C and D in Figure 21(a) and on the LEE SIDE (or downwind) of the person in the water, the helmsman releases the lifesling. The purpose is to wrap the line around the casualty so that the sling can be pulled along to be positioned under the armpits as in Figure 21(b). (With an unconscious victim it may be necessary to make several wrapping turns and then bring him alongside to fit the sling.) The lifesling, of course, has some additional buoyancy, but the real morale booster is that the casualty is again in contact with 'home'. Another tight turn, and the yacht is making its second circle and slowing for the pick-up.

The temptation to start the engine at this stage must be resisted, because the last thing you want is a wrap round the propeller; and *never* go overboard to help for that way lies double jeopardy. With the casualty in the sling, the person on board will only have time to cast off the sheets and let the sails down at the run before considering what to do next. Time and temperature will dictate what follows. With a warm sea, a short ducking and a cheerful casualty it might be a good idea to fetch the bathing or boarding ladder and let him get out by himself. If, on the other hand, the recovered crew member looks pinched and cold, moves sluggishly, and is blue in the face, it is best first to lash him firmly alongside to a cleat or winch and use mechanical or other means to get him out smartly.

One solution is shown in Figure 21(c) where the resourceful rescuer has attached the main sheet to the

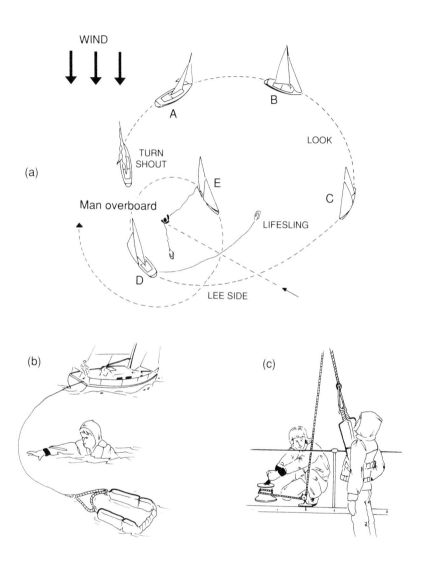

Figure 21 Man overboard: the pick-up

sling and is winching her companion out using the end of the boom as a crane. (The mechanical advantage offered by a pair of blocks makes this feasible; it would not work half as well with a single block.) Launching a half-inflated dinghy and bundling the casualty into it gets him out of the water too, and with some yachts recovery could take place at the stern thereafter. If stuck at this point, and in well-frequented waters, consider making a Mayday call on VHF to get assistance, or signal passing craft by raising and lowering your extended arms in a call for help. Once on board, the rescued crew must be hustled down into the cabin and treated for hypothermia, whether this is liked or not. This means swathing the casualty in blankets or sleeping bags, using a space blanket or applying well-wrapped hot water bottles for slow warming in extreme cases. The treatment for shock is on the same lines: warmth, rest and sips of hot, sweet tea, but absolutely no alcohol.

6 Mooring and anchoring

Picking up a pile mooring

In many Solent rivers, and some Dutch and Baltic ports, the pressure on mooring space is such that steel or wooden piles have been steam-hammered into the mud so that yachts can tie up between them. You may be directed by the harbour master to take your place on a mooring of this type with one or more craft already lying there. The correct technique is to come alongside a boat of your own size and make fast temporarily to it. With the dinghy in the water, one crew member will pay out the warp (and receive an end in due course) while the other paddles the dinghy out to the pile and passes the rope around the welded tube standing out from the pile, or the ring at the bottom of the tube if it is low water and you can get at it easily. Adjust both warps for tension, and then rearrange the lines to the boat next door as springs and breast ropes. The tiresome part is first inflating and then deflating the dinghy, so that a small crew may find it advantageous to carry an LVM dinghy inflator working off the battery, which will inflate and deflate a rubber dinghy in about a minute and a half.

The procedure is a little more complicated when you are the first yacht tying up between piles, and there are two things to do before making fast with the warps. Take the boat close and lie parallel to the posts. If there is a buoyed, or even an unbuoyed, rope between them this is a sign of permanent chains and warps hidden beneath the surface, and an indication that the mooring has a returning owner. I will come to mooring ethics later, but these signs of permanent occupancy make this a less desirable berth than it might otherwise have been, and the wise skipper will look for unencumbered piles with nothing between them. Having found the right pair, this is the time to check whether the wind is stronger than the tide, or vice versa, so that you can decide which of the two piles is the up-wind or the up-tide one.

We will assume that the wind is stronger than the tide, and the yacht motors slowly up to the windward pile where the crew passes the forward warp round the tube or ring. Falling back on the downwind pile in a controlled way, the stern warp is similarly secured and then the tension on both warps is adjusted to get the craft midway between the posts. It is not always this easy, for a perverse law of averages seems to decree that the wind and tide will invariably be at right angles to each other, so that the yacht does *not* fall back agreeably to the second post. What you have to do in such circumstances is secure to the windward pile and fall back *towards* the downwind pile with the dinghy in the water and a warp ready. Do not try to tug the parent craft towards the post; far better to middle the stern warp as it goes round the tube or ring and take the two ends back to the yacht, passing them on board to the second crew member for making fast.

Mooring to a single buoy

A single buoy with a 360° swinging angle is ideal for a cruising yacht on passage that merely wants to tie up for the night and be on its way in the morning. There is, however, a code of ethics that must be observed. The visiting yachtsman is using someone else's property, and has three obligations. Firstly, the chain and mooring should be robust enough to take the pull of the moored yacht. Secondly, as enough people must be on board at all times to move the yacht if the owner returns unexpectedly, it is unlikely that any members of a small crew will get ashore. Thirdly, and most important, it is always wise to get explicit permission to use the mooring if readily available. Where the buoy is near a boatyard or opposite the harbour master's office it is good form to go ashore, obtain consent and pay the appropriate fee. The exception is when a buoy is one of a recognized group of moorings for visitors where a harbour official comes by boat several times a day to collect the fees. What a shorthanded crew must not do, in any circumstances, is to tie up to a buoy and then go away leaving the yacht unattended.

Single mooring buoys are of the three main types shown in Figure 22(a). In Figure 22(a)1, the riding chain leads straight up to a buoy with a metal ring on top, and that ring is a strong hint that you will probably need to pass a warp, or two, through the ring and back on board again to lie off under the push of wind or tide. In Figure 22(a)2, the spherical buoy without a ring looks as though it will have to be brought on deck under the rail to start with, and then the nature of what lies below will dictate what has to be done. A long thin buoy rope will suggest that the attached chain should be hauled in and made fast; a short thin buoy rope followed by a much thicker warp tells you that the latter goes round a winch, bollard or cleat to secure the yacht. Figure 22(a)3 shows the very common type of pick-up buoy that is brought in under the rail and the loop placed around a foredeck fixture. It is good manners to lash the pick-up buoy to the forestay after the loop is secured to tell passing craft and those coming into moorings that you are on a buoy and not at anchor.

Dinghy on the mooring

A two-man crew out for a day's sail will often want to leave a dinghy on their mooring buoy for the return to shore, and there is a recurring problem of it bumping and grinding under the bow of the parent craft when leaving and returning to the buoy. Two solutions are worth trying. With a diverging wind and tide, tie a bucket to the stern of the dinghy and submerge it so that the tide holds the dinghy at a different angle to the more wind-oriented yacht. Alternatively, let the yacht drop back on a long line once the dinghy is made fast to the buoy and tie a float or fender to that line to facilitate a pick-up later. When pulling back to the buoy, the dinghy may be transferred to a fendered position alongside the yacht.

The pick-up

A two-man crew may only be able to spare one pair of hands when making initial contact with the buoy. The usual technique of one person with a boathook hanging on to the buoy, while the other crew member passes the

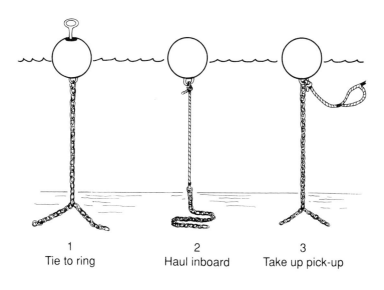

1
Tie to ring

2
Haul inboard

3
Take up pick-up

(a) Mooring buoys

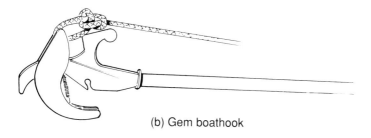

(b) Gem boathook

Figure 22 Mooring buoys and the GEM boathook

warp or pulls the buoy up and under the rail by brute force, cannot be employed unless the helmsman comes forward in good time to help out. Usually, the latter is too busy steering right up to the buoy or alongside it to be available to help at that precise moment, so there are five other possibilities, starting with the one-man mooring hook.

The GEM (or gem) boathook, shown in Figure 22(b), is one of those brilliant ideas from Sweden that makes use of a principle long applied in cloth weaving. Its

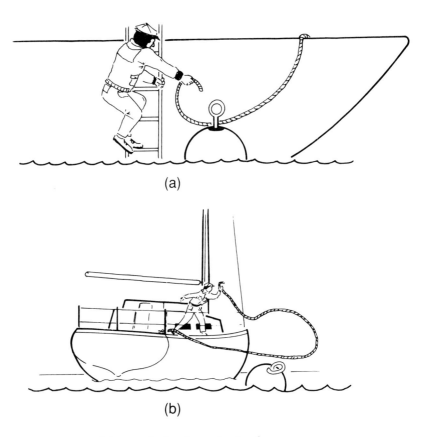

(a)

(b)

Figure 23 Other methods of securing to a buoy

great advantage over ordinary spring-clip boathook fittings is that it brings the rope back on board. The rope is fixed to a shuttle, and when the hook is triggered by the mooring ring on top of the buoy, the shuttle passes through the eye and everything pulls through to leave the rope through the ring and holding the craft on its new mooring. For a small crew, it has the bonus that there is no subsequent wrestling over the bow to get the spring clip off after putting replacement mooring lines through the ring.

It is only fair to say that the GEM boathook works well in calm conditions for boats with a low freeboard. However, with a nodding buoy, a pitching boat and a crew member understandably unwilling to lean out too far over the pulpit, it sometimes happens that the hook cannot be made to close on the ring or handle of the buoy. Two alternatives appear in Figure 23; the solution in Figure 23(a) is one adopted by high-sided craft of the MFV type. The yacht is brought alongside the buoy, and a crew member clinging to a ladder, or lying down at full length on the side deck, threads the warp through the ring and then takes the free end back up to the bow and makes it fast. Figure 23(b) shows the slightly more desperate expedient of coming alongside a buoy and throwing a loop of warp over it. Once the craft has come to rest the warp is tightened to bring the buoy alongside and the ropes that will hold it for the night can be put on.

In really bad conditions, and when there is nothing much to get hold of on the buoy, one solution is to make a lasso with a bowline on the bight and drop it over the buoy so that it tightens around the chain. The disadvantage of this particular operation is that you will almost certainly have to launch the dinghy the next day to tease and loosen the knot, which will have bound and swollen during a night on the mooring. Finally, there is always the case when a plunging sea makes it a hopeless business to get a warp through the ring of a buoy or around it, and the last resource is to launch the dinghy with its outboard so that one crew member makes fast while the other keeps the yacht reasonably stationary near by. There is not much chance of running a free end back on this occasion; better to get a couple of round turns and two half hitches on the ring of the buoy and pull the boat up to make fast properly when *both* crew members are on hand to pass and secure the warps.

Mooring between two buoys

The authorities responsible for moorings in swift-flowing rivers often insist that visiting craft tie to two buoys, to prevent damage as the boats range about with the wind and tide. The method used to take up such a berth is almost identical to that employed when mooring between two piles. When there is a line between buoys it may be treated as a pick-up rope, so that the yacht comes alongside as if mooring to a quay, head to current. Beforehand, put out *two* boathooks so that both crew members can bring the pick-up rope inboard and then rough-lash it to cleats while sorting out more permanent head and stern ropes to the buoys.

Chafe

The strain on warps holding a boat between two buoys is much greater than when lying to a single mooring, and chafe is the great enemy. Previously, chafe was countered by parcelling old canvas round the rope and in the jaws of the fairlead, but current practice is to use stout plastic tubing. The only difficulty is keeping the slippery tubing in place in the fairlead; I usually bore a hole with a red-hot piece of coathanger wire at each end of the tubing, tie a length of cord to each hole with a bowline and then clove-hitch the other end of the cord to the warp so that it will not 'walk' along the rope. Similar protection can be provided by putting tubing on a permanent mooring chain. Of course, this is also a guard against another sort of chafe – that of the chain marking and scarring the hull as the boat shifts to the pressure of wind and tide.

Anchors

You may occasionally see a cruiser up for sale with an inventory that includes one anchor of the lunch hook variety and a short length of tattered warp, but a small crew with safety at the forefront of their minds will know instinctively that this kind of provision is grossly inadequate. The size, number and type of anchors and the amount of chain and warp are matters for careful consideration with no one easy answer. I propose to run through the eight main types of anchor and grade them for suitability as main bower, kedge and second anchor.

The Britany, Danforth and Stockless anchors in Figure 24 are all designed to fit into hawsepipes and are therefore out of the way when voyaging, but ready for instant use. The next two are Bruce and CQR patents, which are difficult to stow so that they tend to live on chocks, in recessed bow lockers, or are put out on the bow roller. The last three are folders: the Sea

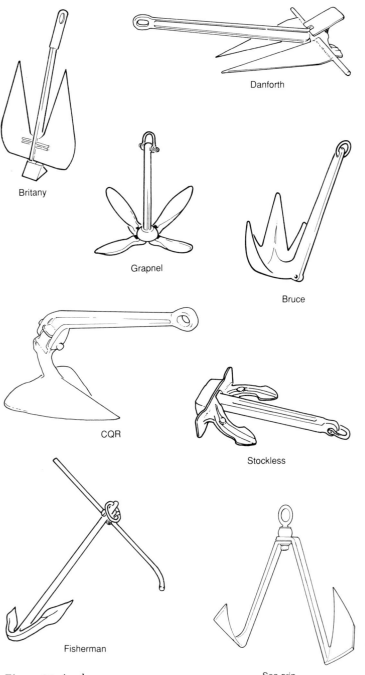

Danforth

Britany

Grapnel

Bruce

CQR

Stockless

Fisherman

Sea grip

Figure 24 Anchors

Grip hinges in half; the Grapnel has leaves that fold inwards; the Fisherman has a stock that pushes through the shank and is lashed parallel to it. This last group – folders – are obvious candidates for kedge anchors, and they would normally be fitted with just a few feet of chain and perhaps 30 metres of anchorplait. A kedge would usually be stowed in an easily accessible locker in the aft part of the yacht.

It is reckoned that a boat needs about one and a half kilograms of anchor weight to every metre of its length, and the table that follows gives an indication of what a lightly manned craft between six and twelve metres overall will require.

Boat length (metres)	Anchor weight (kilograms)	Diameter of chain (a) inches (b) millimetres	
6	9	1/4	
7	10	5/16	8
8	12	3/8	
9	12	3/8	9
10	14	3/8	
11	16	3/8	
12	18	3/8	9

As to length of chain, 60 metres is the least amount to have shackled on the main bower, with 30 metres of chain and 30 of rope on the second working anchor. The rope, by the way, needs to be 20 millimetre nylon or anchorplait with lots of give in it.

A two-man crew has to balance these requirements against their individual physical capacities and, bearing in mind that anchor winches sometimes jam or refuse duty, try putting some rope on the selected size of main anchor and lifting it some six feet or so vertically. If that is all right, add a couple of pounds to stand for clogging seaweed and adhesion from thick mud and try again. With the weight right for you and the boat, begin to think about types of anchor.

Broadly, the Danforth and Britany anchors are good on sand, mud and shingle; the Fisherman holds on rock and in weed; and the Bruce holds well on rock. My own choice for an average summer-cruising yacht would be a 12-kilogram Britany, a 10-kilogram Bruce and a 15-kilogram Fisherman. You may be rather surprised that the very popular CQR anchor does not make the top three; the reason is that although it is a plough anchor with an effective swivelling shank, it will roll out on its side once the 90° change of angle is exceeded. It resets, of course, but never so deeply as before, and there is a tendency for it to 'skate' along the seabed once lifted. American yachtsmen fill the underside of the plough with lead to make the CQR dig in more readily, but as this brings it up to the weight of the more versatile Fisherman the exercise seems rather pointless.

Use of the single anchor

An anchor that is going to work properly has to have a firm grip of the seabed, and to achieve that desirable result a shorthanded crew should *always* approach an anchorage under power. The first two considerations are to get the length of chain right and to plant the anchor in the best spot. One view is that the scope

Figure 25 Swinging circles

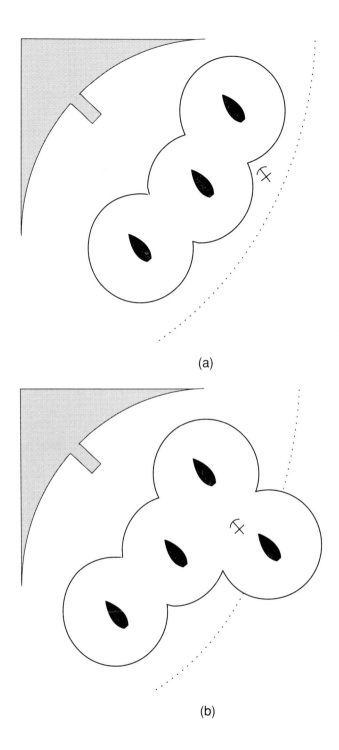

(a)

(b)

must be at least three times the depth at high water, but I think that five times is much more likely.

As for the right spot, the elements are set out in Figure 25. A roadstead on the coast has a shallow shelf suitable for overnight anchoring in three fathoms or so, but the best places are already taken. The three craft are of a similar type and lying head to the offshore wind, so that their swinging circles may be calculated from the distance they lie apart. The best place to drop the anchor is the point where the swinging circles of two of the yachts intersect, marked by an anchor symbol in Figure 25(a).

Lowering the anchor

Shorthanders work on the basis of one to lower and two to raise, so that in the former case the crew at the bow begins by getting the anchor on the bow roller and pulling out three metres or so of chain from the locker, and ranging it on the deck ready to run. At a couple of boat lengths from the dropping point he will ease the anchor over the bow until the crown is almost touching the water and *hold* the chain by hand. (Unless you are constrained by age or disability, it is always better to lower the first part by hand so as to *feel* when the anchor touches bottom.) At the dropping point the bowman makes a sign to the helmsman to indicate that the engine is to go into neutral – usually a levelling side-to-side hand movement – and then lowers the anchor hand-over-hand until a gentle jar tells him that it is on the bottom.

The boat will still have some headway at this point and the bowman will let out some slack fairly rapidly in order to have some chain in hand for putting it on the winch. He then signals the helmsman, perhaps with a lifted forefinger, to go slow astern in a straight line as the chain rattles over the bow roller. A touch on the brake by the bowman when half the chain is out will help the anchor to dig in.

As the agreed scope of cable is approached, the engine is put into neutral and the bowman makes the chain temporarily fast, or flips the pawl over to check its running. The cable will rise towards the horizontal briefly, and the crew at the helm will look about to note transit marks or rough bearings mentally to fix the boat's position. With the chain still secured the engine is put into gear and the helmsman goes slow astern again until the grip of the anchor and the pull of the propeller cancel out, and the craft is stationary with the wake running down the sides of the hull. When satisfied that the anchor is holding, the helmsman gives the bowman a thumbs-up sign to signify that the chain may be permanently secured.

The helmsman now makes a final check by going astern at half speed for thirty seconds or so, then goes into neutral and checks transit marks or bearings. The bowman (without gloves) should *feel* the chain for jerking movements that might signify dragging. When both crew members are satisfied, the anchor ball or anchor light should be hoisted and the depth alarm on the echo sounder set to give warning of a drift to seaward. In Figure 25(b) the yacht has found the right position for the night with the anchor embedded in the three-fathom patch and the hull's swinging circle tangential to the swinging circles of the other windward yachts.

This harmonious relationship is not so easy to achieve with craft of differing windages, since a high-sided motorboat and a deep-lying schooner will respond more to wind and tide respectively so that the swinging circles must be envisaged as irregular. When coming into an anchorage, it pays to put the hook down among craft of your own kind.

Using two anchors

There are three sets of circumstances when two anchors should be used. The first two occur when there is a rising wind and worsening weather with the craft already lying at a single anchor. In Figure 26(a) a yacht lying to a westerly wind on a single anchor receives a forecast of stronger west to north-west winds. The crew then put

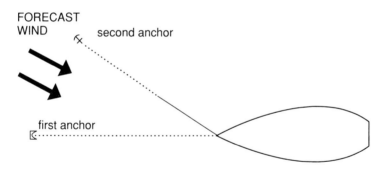

(a) More wind from a different quarter

(b) Back-up anchor: wind from the same quarter

Figure 26 Using two anchors

out a second anchor at about 30° to the first, so that the forecast wind will roughly bisect the pull of both anchors. If the warning is received in good time, the crew can motor out to windward to the second anchor-dropping position in Figure 26(a), but remember that less scope can be obtained when this method is used because of the friction on the seabed of the chain of the first anchor. With the dinghy available, take out the second anchor in the same way as deploying a kedge, but bear in mind these useful shortcuts for a light crew. Take out *all* the chain and warp with you in the dinghy under engine, with the chain and warp stowed in running order and the anchor lightly lashed and over the stern so that a slash with the knife will let it go. Have an extra length of warp with you in case you have misjudged things and have to bend on a little more rope to bring the inboard end back to your companion.

The back-up or tandem arrangement in Figure 26(b) is for when the craft is lying at anchor with the wind increasing but remaining in the same direction. To get it absolutely right, it is as well to raise the single anchor and move around under power while the second is shackled on. Tandem anchors only work well with a straight pull, because if there is a change of wind direction one of the anchors (usually the one nearest the boat) will capsize and act merely as a weight thereafter.

The running moor

The third situation in which two anchors should be used is when a boat needs to find a berth for the night, and the tides are strong during the flood and ebb. In these circumstances the running moor

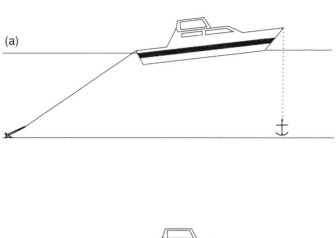

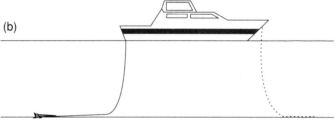

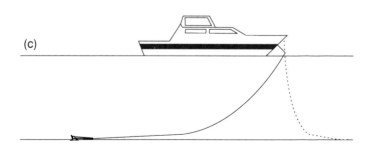

Figure 27 The running moor

will serve to keep her in position. In Figure 27(a) the motor yacht drops her kedge as she comes up to the anchorage and runs on the full length of the cable, pulling up with a jerk at its extremity and bedding the anchor in firmly. The main bower is then lowered, and the yacht motors slowly astern paying out chain from the bow while the crew tends the kedge rope and makes sure it does not lift or tangle in the propellers. In the final stage, the yacht comes to a halt midway between the two anchors, as in Figure 27(b), and the crew who has been tending the kedge detaches the inboard end of its rope and carries it forward, tying it to the main chain cable. Paying out a couple of feet of main cable brings about the position in Figure 27(c). The yacht is moored between two anchors, but pivots at the bow to wind and tide and has a restricted swinging circle. The great advantage of the running moor is that a lightly manned yacht does not have to keep an anchor watch when moored in a narrow channel with strong tides or currents.

Raising the anchor

Sailing an anchor out of the ground is often given a paragraph in books on seamanship, but so far as the two-man crew is concerned the engine should be brought into the equation every time. There are a number of points to consider when raising the anchor, and the first is that signals will have to be made by the foredeck crew to the helmsman. As the boat goes slow ahead the bowman works the winch in bursts: taking in chain; halting at intervals to point to where the chain is 'growing' and where the helmsman is to steer. These pauses, with the pawl engaged, will also allow him to get his breath back and stow any chain that has not slithered down the pipe into the locker. At the up-and-down stage when the chain is vertical, the foredeck crew will lift an arm skywards to call for neutral, and may have to wait a few seconds for a wave to lift the bow that odd inch or two that gets the anchor out of its grave. With the crown awash, the person on the foredeck will make a two-handed pausing gesture and beckon the second crewman forward. Two are better than one when the anchor has to be lifted in over the bow, and even hawsepipe-fitting anchors need twisting in the hole to get them straight so that heavy-duty gloves are a must for both persons involved. Finally, keep a bucket of seawater handy for washing mud and weed off the anchor as it comes home; it is easier to clean off at this stage than to wait for the next port of call, when the mud will have dried and caked solid on the flukes.

7 Making harbour

Lowering sails

During the final approach to a port the sails have to come down and be stowed *before* you begin to manœuvre under engine; the headsail needs muzzling first. In a lightly manned yacht one person will be aft keeping the hull head to wind, with short bursts of slow ahead alternating with neutral, while the sole foredeck hand will need some simple mechanical aids to help the job along. First of these is the downhaul. This is not an elaborate device, just a cord made fast to the head of the sail and threaded inside the hanks or snaphooks parallel to the forestay (see Figure 28). Halfway down, the cord emerges from the hanks and loops across to the eye at the clew. The second device is a spliced eye at the free end of the halyard, carefully calculated to go round the barrel of the winch when the snap shackle at the other end of the halyard is fast to the pulpit.

Before describing how the headsail comes down, it may be instructive to justify these departures from normal sail-handling practice. The orthodox view is that while the mainsail *has* to come down head to wind, the foresail may be brought down on any heading. However, as shorthanders cannot spare a man both to slack off the halyard and lean out to gather in the sail, it makes sense to drop head to wind so that the lower

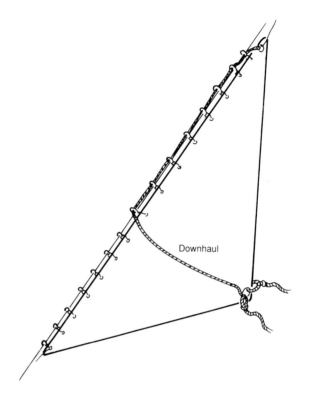

Downhaul

Figure 28 A downhaul

part of the headsail falls on to the foredeck. Similarly, the spliced eye on the free end of the halyard enables the foredeck worker to secure the spliced end to the winch drum on the mast *before* moving forward to gather in the bulk of the sail. The reason for using a splice and not a bowline is that a spliced eye leads to about a 10 per cent loss in the strength of the rope, a knot up to 40 per cent.

With the yacht head to wind and the sheets loosened by the helmsman, the forward crew member takes position on the port side of the mast, removes the headsail halyard from the cleat and slackens the turns on the winch drum. The tension being off, the weight and flutter of the sail will bring down several feet of the lowest part of the sail to the deck, and when the same crewman takes the halyard right off the drum the result is a few more feet of sail down. (In the case of yachts with halyards leading aft it is the helmsman who lets go the halyard and the foredeck hand who worries the sail down.) The spliced loop is placed over the winch drum, and the crewman steps forward to grab hold of the clew and downhaul to pull the remainder of the sail on to the foredeck. Yachts with large crews bag their headsails there and then, but the shorthander will usually bundle them up in a long sausage on the guardrail and tie them there with pieces of cord or elastic left clove-hitched on the rail for this purpose. The helmsman assists his companion by keeping tension on the appropriate sheet as the sail is secured. Naturally, self-furling headsails eliminate the need for any foredeck work (either hoisting or lowering) and are a boon for the shorthanded crew.

Lowering and securing the mainsail is initially easier, since the person at the starboard side of the mast can slacken the halyard with one hand and pull the slides down with the other. As in the case of the headsail, the free end of the halyard has a loop so that when the sail is down the halyard can be hooked to the cleat and forgotten about. The task is, of course, child's play with a full-battened mainsail and lazyjacks where the lowered sail flakes itself on the boom, but with a traditional mainsail the crew has to be quick and positive in making it fast. With the sail down, the crew starts by inserting a long sail tie through the cringle, the hole in the headboard or the shackle securing the halyard, passing it round the bundle of sail *and* the boom and knotting the tie with a reef knot. Then, with the other crew member bringing in the main sheet to give a rigid boom, he moves away from the mast to stretch the leech of the sail along the boom and piles the loose sail on to it. Reaching below the boom to grasp a fold of the sail, he makes a trough and pushes the loose sail into it, then piles the resultant sausage on top of the boom and holds it with his chest and one arm while fishing in pockets for more sail ties. Passing two or three round the bundle and tying them is enough to hold the sail until a harbour stow can be made following berthing.

A quick and easy alternative to secure the sail is two parallel lengths of elastic line strung permanently beneath the boom between the mast and the boom end. The lengths are seized at two-foot intervals and between each seizing are hooks which allow the elastic to be drawn up on each side of the boom and hooked together at the top, holding the bulging sail in place.

Warps and fenders

In most cases a cruising yacht will not know exactly where it will moor or what side to, so it is a good idea to have four warps ready – one on each bow and one for each quarter. The two-man crew will rig the warps ready for instant deployment with one end made fast to a cleat, the rope then led through the rails and fairlead, looped over the rail and coiled on deck. A fifth warp known by a number of names – breast rope, one-line motor mooring, spring line or gob rope – should be ready amidships. This is a short rope, about the length of the boat, with a spliced eye at one end, and essentially it is for holding the boat temporarily still by its middle while the two-man crew work at both ends.

While on the subject of ropes, this is an opportunity to remind shorthanders about colour-coding. Much time will be saved when groping in lockers for warps if they have coloured whipping at the ends to show their purpose – perhaps red for long warps, blue for shorter springs and breast lines, and yellow for the gob rope.

Fenders come next, and this is the time to question the received wisdom that says fenders should always be hung vertically and suspended from a lanyard clove-hitched to the top rail or wire. Many berthing places have piling with vertical ribs, or pontoons in sections with gaps between, so that it sometimes makes sense to hang fenders horizontally from two lanyards when making initial contact, as in Figure 29. In most cases protection for the hull is required just above the waterline, and horizontally fitted fenders give more

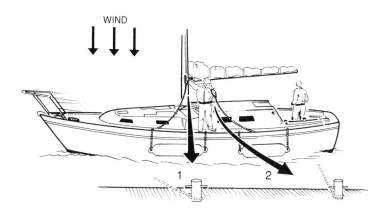

Figure 29 Coming alongside

coverage low down, as a glance at any professional waterman's craft will confirm.

Figure 29 shows two fenders, and this is the bare minimum per side; three are better and an additional bow fender and spare in the cockpit for emergencies better still. Fenders should be secured round the *base* of the stanchions to give more holding purchase for the lanyards than can be provided by merely knotting them on the top rail or wire. They should be put on well before coming up to the berth, for only the most insecure of yachtsmen worries about being under way with fenders out in harbour.

Coming alongside, onshore wind, no tide

Figure 29 shows the basics of an easy berthing with a favourable wind blowing the yacht gently on to an empty jetty with the tide neutral. The warps that were readied earlier on the port side have been gathered together by the foredeck hand, who has them ready to drop over the bollards. (Note here that like all experienced shorthanders, the crew of this particular yacht have had an eye spliced to one end of each warp. It has a dual function: for dropping over a bollard as on this occasion, and for instant fixing to an inboard cleat when the other end has to be used.) The helmsman's job is not, as in the case of fully manned yachts, to put the boat between the bollards but to centre it on the one in the middle of Figure 29. As the boat nudges the jetty the crew member handling the warps will drop the forewarp marked 1 over the centre bollard, jump ashore, and walk the other rope marked 2 to the right-hand bollard. With a very low, or a very high, berthing place, it might be necessary for the crewman with the warps to be ready outside the guard rails to jump ashore or reach for the first bollard.

The boat is astern of its eventual position and the helmsman, now finished with tiller and engine, will be able to assist in repositioning the boat by handling the stern warp from inboard while the companion tends the forewarp and bears off as necessary. In this instance, the forward warp will eventually go on a bollard out of the illustration to the left, while springs are put on the central bollard to achieve the correct mooring pattern. So much for the easy part: now for a rather more tricky berthing problem.

Coming alongside, offshore wind, awkward tide

A common predicament is set out in Figure 30(a), where a yacht is berthing on the lee side of a crowded pontoon with a strong wind blowing it off and a feebler tide tending to push it past the berth. Slow backing and filling is not going to work here, and the turn into the wind will require full power and rudder followed by fierce astern to stop the boat hitting the pontoon a nasty clout. The preparations *must* include putting on the bow fender at the correct height, having two other fenders ready on the port bow plus one further aft, the headrope ready for use, and the gob rope or spring line made fast amidships with its looped end secured lightly forward (by cotton, for example) to the outside of the pulpit.

As the bow comes in to the pontoon and the water boils with the engine full astern, the crew member with the bow rope should make a flying leap and put

110

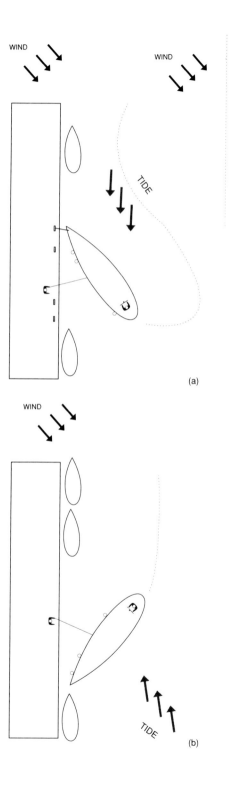

(a)

(b)

the warp over or round and round the cleat or bollard. He or she then tears the loop of the gob rope from its light lashing to the pulpit and, before the bow swings out, takes the loop two bollards aft and drops it over. This is the state of play in Figure 30(a) where the gob rope fastened amidships and the bow warp are holding the boat until the stern warp and springs are put on. The rest is mere hauling, with the crew on the pontoon standing by to receive the stern rope from the helmsman. In very strong winds the cockpit winch may need to be used to pull the stern in, and the crew will certainly have to slacken the bow warp as the hull comes parallel to the pontoon.

Figure 30(b) shows the other side of the coin. The tide is stronger than the wind, which means that while an up-tide approach is correct, the wind will take the stern off once the boat is stationary. At the time the foredeck hand makes the jump ashore to secure the bow warp the yacht will begin to swing to the push of the wind; smart work with the gob rope will halt this movement and the bows-in position can be held until the stern rope is passed across. Of course, with an unencumbered pontoon this manoeuvre can be made more easily, with the yacht coming directly alongside and securing with the stern warp first as slow headway is maintained, and the bowman racing ahead with the forewarp to ensnare the chosen bollard.

This action is also appropriate in locks where a following wind has to be countered by securing first by the stern to avoid the hideous embarrassment of ending up with the bow touching one wall and the stern the other.

Figure 30 Bow in

Berthing with warps

Sometimes only the harbour's most inaccessible berth is on offer, and a possible scenario is outlined in Figure 31(a). A strong spring tide is running into a basin after the gates have been opened, and the wind is behind it. The harbour master suggests that you take up berth D in Figure 31(a), but as you draw near it is apparent that there is no room to turn and face wind and tide in the approach or in the space between two sets of moored yachts. Backing in seems to be fraught with uncertainty because of steps which are in the way, so the first action is to come alongside the moored boat marked X and secure temporarily to it to plan the next move.

A look round confirms your first diagnosis that turning is likely to damage your boat or others, and there is still too little space to be sure that engine manœuvres will get you out of trouble. The correct solution is to warp the yacht down the line of boats, using the wind and tide to keep it off them, but the question is how to do it with just two people. The key is to allot *two* warps to each person thereby ensuring that one is always attached while the other is being shifted.

In Figure 31(a) the taut warps are shown, and in moving from position A to B both crew are at the stern with lines to X and Y. As the yacht moves down the three moored craft the next set of lines run to Y and the quay, and finally when position D is reached the normal berthing lines may be put out. Once the first pair of warps have been set to take the strain in position B it is preferable for both crew to be on the moored yachts with their individual pairs of warps – securing one to a cleat or fixture, carrying the other to the next boat and making it fast, then returning to

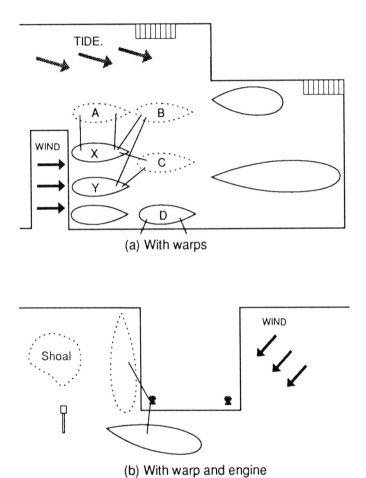

(a) With warps

(b) With warp and engine

Figure 31 Berthing with warps, and with warp and engine

release the first, and so on. Tedious it may be, but this is the only safe way to berth with warps in a confined space. Rudder and engine have no part to play in this manœuvre.

Berthing with warp and engine

Another form of berthing with a strong beam wind involves the use of a warp and the engine. The essentials appear in Figure 31(b) where the gob rope, attached amidships, swings the boat into a berth round a corner. The yacht halts first in the lee of a pier out of the wind and secures the gob rope to a bollard. Pivoting on this line, it is able to motor ahead and turn short to secure to the pier without running the risk of going aground. A similar technique might be employed when leaving a berth and wanting to hold on to the pier to stop the yacht being blown into the shallows.

The Mediterranean moor

The pressure on mooring space nowadays means that the Mediterranean method of securing yachts seems likely to spread to northern Europe. This method embraces four separate variations in technique. Put simply, the most usual technique involves the yacht dropping its anchor and backing up to moor with stern warps to a quay – but, as you may imagine, that is not the whole story. To begin with, engines do not give of their best in reverse; it is difficult to know exactly where the anchors and chains of other crafts are lying when going in backwards; and your own anchor does not bite properly unless a good speed is maintained on the run-in to the berth. For these reasons I suggest that the procedure set out in Figure 32 should be adhered to.

In Figure 32 the shorthanded yacht makes its approach to the quay bows-on, dropping its anchor clear of the others already on the bottom and going straight in until half the estimated scope of chain is out. Keeping pressure on the chain to bed the anchor well in, the yacht comes round 180° in a tight turn and then reverses in slowly, paying out more chain as it goes. Within a few feet of the quay the helmsman should slow right down and, keeping the chain under tension, continue going astern very slowly, giving the foredeck crew a chance to secure the chain at the bow and move aft. (Things are much easier for two when the boat has an electric winch controlled from the cockpit: then the helmsman can tend to the anchor and the deck crew concentrate on getting warps ashore.) The quay jumper makes the flying leap as the helmsman juggles with throttle and gear lever to keep the boat stationary a foot or so from the quay. Two warps, one from each quarter, are usual, but if there is a surge in the harbour they may be supplemented by crosswarps to check sideways movement (yacht Z in Figure 32 has these extra warps in place). At night, slacken the warps and take in some chain to keep a safe distance from the quay, moving back in by day. The stern gangway should also be taken in at night to discourage light-fingered visitors.

116

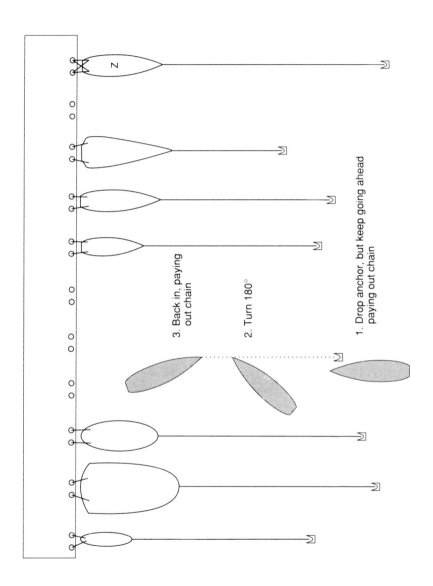

Figure 32 The Mediterranean moor

The Greek moor

In this version of the Mediterranean moor a boat drops a kedge over the stern on the run-in and secures by bow warps, with three distinct advantages in shallow harbours. The risk of grounding on the debris that accumulates at the foot of sea walls is reduced; the possibility of damage to stern gear when a swell runs in is eliminated; and privacy is enhanced. The disadvantage is that many modern yachts are fine-lined at the bow and it is difficult to find enough room to plant your feet when disembarking and boarding, while pulpits have a forward rake that makes getting aboard a knee-cracking exercise.

Ground chain moorings

These are of two types. In the first there is a massive ground chain running parallel to the quay with buoys attached. The anchor is not required, and the whole art is in getting a bow warp through the ring of the buoy as the boat slides back at right angles to the quay. Shorthanders will need the GEM boathook described in Chapter 6 to snare the buoy, and the solitary foredeck worker will thereafter have to gallop aft to make his leap for the quay with the stern warps. Fortunately, most Mediterranean harbours are crowded so that it is often possible to go alongside another vessel and tie up briefly after the bow rope is secured to the buoy. Then one crew member can make his way to the quay via the boat alongside while the second, freed from duty at helm and engine controls, can coil and throw the stern warps ashore.

The second ground chain device is the *chêne morte*, which is part chain and part rope and lies at right angles to the quay. There is one per berth, and from the yacht there is nothing to see save a ringbolt in the vertical face of the quay with a rope vanishing into the water beneath it. The yacht comes in astern as usual, and the first thing to do is either tie up to another boat as in the previous paragraph, or put out a pair of stern warps to the quay, maintaining position with the engine. The crew member who has leaped ashore to make these stern warps fast now has to fish up the light rope attached to the ring on the wall.

This is not as simple as it sounds, and there are three things to bear in mind. Often the rope is a long way down so you will need a boathook; the mooring is inevitably encrusted with sharp growths so gloves are recommended; and you have to get back on board, or summon the helmsman, to follow the rope to its end. Shuffling forward and passing the rope through your hands as it comes out of the water, you will eventually come to a massive loop of chain or rope, and this goes round the bitts, cleat or anchor winch to hold the bow. The stern warps may now be adjusted to achieve the correct distance for the gangway. Naturally, picking up the *chêne morte* entails ample fendering on both sides *and* the stern, and crew have to be extremely careful not to let the rope foul the propeller as it is drawn up. The best method is to get it to one side and pull it up between your boat and the next one.

Dinghy work

It used to be said that a ship was known by her boats, and it is certainly the case that the quality of dinghy handling in harbour is an index of a shorthanded crew's performance at sea. Many dinghies are made to carry either one or three people, and trim is vital when two are embarking. The rower gets in first and *sits* down at once close to where he will be rowing – usually in the forepart of the dinghy. He holds it tightly alongside the parent craft while the second crew boards and sits down aft. As has been emphasized before in this book, a dinghy belonging to shorthanders should have two painters – one at the bow and one at the stern – and both will still be secured at this stage.

The crew should be wearing lifejackets and keep their fingers off the gunwale. The passenger in the stern seat casts off his painter, and the rower extends the outboard oar. As the bow painter is released, the rower gives a light push, ships the inboard oar and then *pulls against the wind and/or tide to judge its strength.* The rower gauges the offset of these forces, and rows obliquely to shore to counteract them. On the return trip, with wind and tide unchanged, the rower may have to work upstream in slack water before slanting across to return to the yacht.

Disembarkation at a slip is best done with boots on so that one crew member – usually the rower – can get out and stand ankle-deep. The buoyant bow of the dinghy can then be carried a little way up the slip so that the passenger may get out dry-shod. At a public landing place, tie the oars and make the painter fast under those of boats already moored there. Beware of tying to ladders when a long visit ashore is con-templated lest the tide retreats to leave your dinghy dangling. If using an outboard engine, make sure not only that the clamps are tight but have a short piece of stout cord joining engine and transom.

On returning to the yacht, draw alongside the shrouds and make the bow painter fast before falling back to the boarding position and securing the stern line. Again, the rower should hold the dinghy tightly alongside as the passenger clambers out. The rower hands up the pump, oars, rowlocks and engine for stowage on board, leaving the dinghy absolutely empty. (In handing up the outboard the length of safety lanyard should be used to secure the engine to the pulpit first.) The dinghy should be left empty because if the boat flips over in the wind during the night, or sinks because of a leak, the gear will be safe. In any case it will have a longer life if stored away from dew and salt-bearing wind. The dinghy painters are now unlashed and the dinghy led aft to lie on a short scope astern for the night.

Harbour cares

A small crew should always be looking ahead, and what follows is in the form of an *aide-mémoire* about the sensible steps that may be taken in harbour between legs of a voyage. Heavy weather may detain you, and while a responsible two-man crew will always wait for a favourable forecast, there may well be a choppy sea outside even when the wind is down. It makes good sense, therefore, to put a deep reef in the mainsail and prepare a small headsail in harbour before leaving; it is easy to shake reefs out or change to a larger sail, but not so easy to cope the other way round in a tumbling sea. Change the engine oil, even though the stipulated period has yet to expire, because there may be a lot of motor sailing in the conditions following a gale. Get the trim right with heavies, like books, amidships and light things like sleeping bags stowed in the ends. Cultivate a primary separation of below-deck gear by function, for joint knowledge of where to start looking for a spanner or a scraper is better than the practice followed in so many yachts, where all the drawers and lockers have contents labels, but nothing within matches the description.

So much for the inside: now the outside of the boat. A long-handled hull scrubber will enable a two-man crew to clean the hull down to a foot or more below the waterline and save a mid-season haul-out. Donning a shallow-water diving set and taking a look at the propeller, rudder and keel will put your mind at rest about any deficiencies in that direction. Fenders convey dirt from quayside to hull and need a scrub in rotation, while warps require freshening in the nip to keep down chafe.

The key decision to sail or not to sail is not just a matter of forecasts and millibars; a small crew seeking the right answer can do no better than leave their boat for a walk to the end of the pier. There is no substitute for looking at the sea and feeling the wind on your cheek to determine what shall be done on the morrow.

Other Adlard Coles titles of interest

Cruising Under Sail Eric Hiscock
ISBN 0 229 11765 1   £14.99

A major work, covering every practical aspect of
cruising for the beginner and expert alike. A sensible
approach to sound seamanship.

Cruising: A Manual for Small Cruiser Sailing (4th edn)
J D Sleightholme
ISBN 0 229 11772 4   £11.95

A comprehensive and commonsense guide to offshore
cruising for those who have grasped the fundamentals.

Singlehanded Sailing Richard Henderson
ISBN 0 229 11854 2   £17.95

Covers the whole spectrum of singlehanded sailing on
coastal and ocean voyages. Much useful information
for the shorthander.

Cruising with Children Gwenda Cornell
ISBN 0 229 11790 2   £13.95

The book that thousands of sailing parents have been
looking for. Full of practical advice.

Strong Wind Sailing Richard Henderson
ISBN 0 229 11832 1   £7.95

Strategies, tactics and techniques for sailing in winds of force 5-8 are explained.

Instant Weather Forecasting Alan Watts
ISBN 0 229 11724 4   £4.95

24 colour cloud photographs assist weather forecasting.

Instant Wind Forecasting Alan Watts
ISBN 0 229 11830 5   £5.95

Colour photographs enable wind predictions to be made.

Channel Crossings Around Britain Peter Cumberlidge
ISBN 0 229 11852 6   £16.95

An invaluable reference book for anyone planning to set off for foreign waters. A passage-making guide for over 16 routes around Britain.

Using Your Decca Pat Langley-Price & Philip Ouvry
ISBN 0 229 11853 4   £7.99

Explains in layman's terms how to get the best from your Decca set.

Radar Mate C A G Brooke & Captain S Dobell
ISBN 1 229 11789 9   £7.95

Designed to help readers identify the images shown on a radar screen.

All Weather Yachtsman Peter Haward
ISBN 0 229 11867 4   £8.99

A collection of the author's experiences of delivering
boats in a variety of weather conditions and seasons.
An entertaining as well as instructive book.

Ocean Cruising on a Budget Anne Hammick
ISBN 0 229 11863 1   £12.99

A guide for prospective sailors wishing to make an
extended cruise on a limited budget. Full of down to
earth practical advice.

Knots in Use Colin Jarman
ISBN 0 229 11712 0   £4.95

A pocket book of useful and practical knots, bends,
whippings and splices with excellent photographs and
clear diagrams.

Sailing Tips: 1000 Labour Saving Ideas William Burr
ISBN 0 229 11869 0   £5.99

Quick and easy solutions to a variety of everyday
sailing difficulties.

All these books should be available at your local
bookshop or chandlery. In case of difficulty write to:

Adlard Coles Nautical
A & C Black (Publishers) Ltd
Howard Road
Eaton Socon
Huntingdon
CAMBS
PE19 3EZ

Index